Natural Reason

American University Studies

Series V
Philosophy

Vol. 4

PETER LANG
New York · Berne · Frankfort on the Main · Nancy

Gerard Casey

Natural Reason

A Study of the Notions of Inference, Assent, Intuition, and First Principles in the Philosophy of John Henry Cardinal Newman

PETER LANG
New York · Berne · Frankfort on the Main · Nancy

Library of Congress Cataloging in Publication Data

Casey, Gerard, 1951–
Natural reason.

(American University Studies. Series V, Philosophy,
ISSN 0739-6392; v. 4)
Bibliography: p.
1. Newman, John Henry, 1801–1890 – Knowledge, Theory of.
2. Knowledge, Theory of – History – 19th century. I. Title.
II. Series.
B1649.N474C37 1984   121'.092'4   83-49092
ISBN 0-8204-0078-5

CIP-Kurztitelaufnahme der Deutschen Bibliothek

Casey, Gerard:
Natural reason: a study of the notions of inference,
assent, intuition, and first principles in the
philosophy of John Henry Cardinal Newman / Gerard
Casey. – New York; Berne; Frankfort on the Main;
Nancy: Lang, 1984.
(American University Studies: Ser. 5, Philosophy;
Vol. 4)
ISBN 0-8204-0078-5

NE: American University Studies / 05

Printed by Lang Druck, Inc., Liebefeld/Berne (Switzerland)

TO MY

FATHER AND MOTHER

THE BEST OF ALL POSSIBLE TEACHERS

ACKNOWLEDGEMENTS

I take this opportunity to thank Professor Ralph McInerny for his help and encouragement. I also wish to thank the Philosophy Department of the University of Notre Dame for supporting me, both morally and financially, while I was a student there. Acknowledgement is due to the computer center of the University of Notre Dame and the computer center of The Catholic University of America for their provision of the word-processing facilities which made this book possible. Finally, I wish to thank my wife Patricia Brophy, and my sons Brendan and Eoghan, for being standing reminders that life is larger than philosophy.

PREFACE

This book is intended to be an exploration of some themes in religious epistemology via an examination of the writings of one philosopher: John Henry Cardinal Newman. "Why Newman?" one might ask. My reasoning for focussing on Newman is that I am convinced that many topics currrently of interest to philosophers (such as the justification of religious belief, the relation of Faith to Reason, the possibility of a 'naturalistic' epistemology, etc.) are dealt with by Newman in interesting and original ways. Although this book is primarily an exegetical study of some central Newmanian notions, it is my hope that it may make a contribution to contemporary discussions of these and other issues.

The basic thesis of the book is that Newman's notion of Natural Inference is equivocal: the object of the book is to show that this equivocation exists and to explore its philosophical ramifications. In the first chapter, I clarify the relationship between formal, informal and natural inference. The concept of

´natural inference´ is shown to be equivocal since it connotes two distinct acts of the mind, namely, the limiting case of informal inference and intuition.   In the second chapter I begin by distinguishing assent from certitude.   Then I trace the notion of ´intuition´ through Newman´s works.   I perceive it as having two distinct aspects;   one actively generative (instinct), the other actively receptive (intuition). The notion of simple assent is clarified and is shown to be associated with natural inference in both its forms. I claim, however, that while natural inference, as the limiting case of informal inference, is really distinct from its concomitant simple assent, natural inference, as instinct, is not.

In the third chapter I examine the relationship of inference to assent. In the course of the examination I consider several critical accounts of the nature of this relationship and I conclude that it is, in Newman´s words, primarily a matter of a "change in the order of viewing" a proposition. In the fourth chapter I apply the findings of the earlier chapters to the central notion of a ´first principle.´ Just as there were two kinds of natural inference, so also there are two kinds of first principle, absolute first principles and relative first principles. Absolute first principles are associated with natural inference qua intuition; relative first principles are associated with natural inference qua the limiting case of informal inference.

The book concludes with a brief discussion of the role of first principles in Newman's thought. In regard to the problem of choosing rationally between competing and irreconcilable sets of first principles, I claim that although Newman does not provide us with a set of conditions sufficient to effect such a choice, he does provide us with some pragmatic tests which render our choice of first principles rational. Ultimately, however, Newman has to allow for the compossibility of sets of first principles which are both equi-rational and mutually incompatible.

TABLE OF CONTENTS

CHAPTER 1

INFERENCE

In this chapter, I am going to provide a basic exposition of Newman's account of inference in which I shall try to display Newman's thought on the matter as perspicuously as possible. The purpose of this exposition is to provide a brief account of Newman's thought on this important matter so as to facilitate the discussion of the relationship between inference and assent which is the topic of the third chapter. During the course of the chapter, four facts will emerge:

1. Formal, informal and natural inference form a continuum in terms of conscious mediation.

2. Formal inference is logically distinct from both informal and natural inference.

3. Informal inference and natural inference are distinguishable only in terms of degrees of conscious mediation.

4. The term 'Natural Inference' is used to signify two quite distinct acts of the mind; (1) a limiting case of informal inference, and (2)

an intuition.

Formal Inference

Inference in general is characterized by Newman as the conditional acceptance of a proposition. There are many passages scattered throughout the Grammar of Assent which serve to make this point.[1] All these statements as to what inference is imply a contrast with assent, which is characterized as being the unconditional acceptance of a proposition. Inference and assent can thus be defined reciprocally. Since I shall be discussing the nature of the relationship of inference to assent in the third chapter I shall leave the critical discussion of the nature of ´conditionality´ until then. Here, I shall be concerned with discovering what inference is when considered in itself.

For the purposes of this chapter we can take inference to be synonymous with reasoning.

> We reason when we hold this by virtue of that;
> whether we hold it as evident or as approximat-
> ing or tending to be evident, in either case we
> so hold it because of holding something else to
> be evident or tending to be evident.[2]

Reasoning is a very ordinary and common human activity.

As it occurs in the "state of nature" we apprehend it to be more a simple act than a process or series of acts. In the case of natural inference, which is reasoning in the state of nature, the antecedent and consequent are directly associated; there is no recognition of the medium connecting them. Such natural reasoning is effortless and unconscious, rather like the operations of sense and memory.[3] However, despite (or perhaps because of) its spontaneity natural reasoning is not without fault. In this it also resembles sense and memory, for as our senses sometimes deceive us and our memory sometimes fails, so too does our reasoning capacity lapse from time to time. The melancholy facts are that one man differs from another, one man differs from himself at different times and even when all are agreed and a consensus is reached, it is still possible for the consensus to fall short of the truth. As a result of our individual and communal failings, it is desirable to examine the process of reasoning with a view to discovering a method which "may act as a common measure between mind and mind."[4]

There is also another reason which leads us to try and develop a canon of reasoning. This is the suspicion, derived from the constructive activities of our minds, that the "summa rerum" is one whole, constructed according to definite principles and laws. If we could gain knowledge of the universal or the general, this knowledge would facilitate our ability to reason about particulars. This canonical method of reasoning will have two aspects:

1. Investigative: whereas before the possession of this method we were confined to the solo exercise of our reasoning powers concerning the investigation of things, now that we possess this method we may investigate things conjointly with others.

2. Juridicial: again, whereas once we had simply to rely solely on our individual judgement in assessing the success or failure of our undertakings, now we can use the common measure as a standard by which to judge along with others. We are thus secured against the more egregious personal blunders and saved from a slavish reliance on "the capricious _ipse dixit_

of authority."[5]

Newman points to geometry and algebra as instances of such investigative and juridicial methods in specific areas. Within these areas these methods allow us to escape from the limitations of our individuality. According to Newman, logical inference is simply another such method, differing from geometry and algebra not in kind but in degree. Whereas geometry and algebra are limited to specific areas of inquiry, logical inference is more ambitious and is impatient of any restrictions on its subject matter. Just as geometry and algebra allow us to transcend our individual limitations, so also does logical inference.

> Now, without external symbols to mark out and to steady its course, the intellect runs wild; but with the aid of symbols, as in algebra, it advances with precision and effect. Let then our symbols be words: let all thought be arrested and embodied in words. Let language have a monopoly of thought; and thought go for only so much as it can show itself to be worth in language. Let every prompting of the intellect be ignored, every momentum of argument be disowned, which is unprovided with an equivalent wording, as its ticket for sharing in the common search after truth. Let the authority of nature, common-sense experience, genius, go for nothing. Ratiocination, thus restricted, and put into grooves, is what I have called inference, and the science, which is its regulating principle, is Logic.[6]

This striking passage is worth reflecting on as it contains what Newman obviously considers to be a key element in his account, namely, a sharp distinction between mental and verbal reasoning. Formal inference is verbal. It is "thought arrested in language." As such, it contrasts with both informal inference and natural inference, both of which are non-verbal to some degree. It is my contention that Newman is wrong in insisting upon such a sharp dichotomy between types of inference. Indeed, he is close to being inconsistent as one of his goals is to show the complementarity of formal inference and informal inference. Rather than its being the case that inference can be divided along mental/verbal lines, I claim that Newman's real thesis is that inference is a continuum, with informal inference being its norm and formal inference and natural inference being its limiting cases. What locates a piece of inference at a particular place on the continuum is its degree of consciousness or verbalizability. Reasoning which is completely explicit or conscious is formal inference (or rather, formal inference is its limiting case): reasoning which is completely inexplicit or unconscious is natural inference (or rather, natural inference is its limiting case).

Formal inference is what Newman has in mind in this passage. What is it that restricts ratiocination and puts it into grooves? Language.

Verbal reasoning of whatever kind, as opposed to mental, is what I mean by inference, which differs from logic only as logic is its scientific form.[7]

It will be remembered that our canonical method of reasoning was supposed to fulfill two functions, namely to provide a common measure by which joint investigation could proceed and to supply a test or standard by which to judge the results of such investigation. Insofar as inference can be expressed fully in language these two goals can be achieved. However, if it is the case that not all inference can be fully verbalized, then we may expect there to be a failure to attain these two goals corresponding to the degree of inexpressibility of the inference.

Inference, as conditional, is not so much concerned with propositions per se as with their comparison. Now languages as they exist in their natural state are invariably messy, being infested with idiosyncratic idioms and ambiguous connotations.[8] If our undertaking is to compare propositions then it is of considerable help if the words of the proposition have a simple, definite, and narrow meaning. The more the words of the propositions are emptied of concreteness, the more is such comparison facilitated.[9] To put it briefly, in inference, words tend towards symbols as their limit: in arithmetic, algebra, and geometry, symbols mean precisely what they are defined to mean; nothing more, nothing less. Reasoning erected on such a base can be supremely cogent and unerring. The same holds true of Aristotelian argumentation insofar as it is conducted by means of symbols.

Within the realm of the abstract, logic is demonstrative and incontrovertible. But when it comes to deal with concrete matters the inferential force of logic suffers a decline from demonstration to probability. The reason for this decline is twofold:

1. In any inference there are assumed premises

2. The conclusion of an inference is always abstract.

If the premisses of a given inference are called into question then we must perforce appeal to another set of inferences of which the disputed premisses are conclusions. If the premisses of these inferences are, in turn, called into question we must find some more inferences, etc. In the case of syllogistic arguments with a minimum of two premisses, the rate of increase in the number of premisses is obviously geometrical. Is this retrogression terminable? Yes, according to Newman. At some point in our journey we will arrive at what he calls ´first principles.´ These are "the recondite sources of all knowledge."[10] There is a serious problem with first principles according to Newman and it is this: formal inference can provide no common measure of mind with respect to them. This is obviously the case since they are the ultimate source and foundation of all inferences and so cannot be the conclusion of any inferential process.[11] It is at this level that the real problem of attaining to truth lies, and not in the arrangement of syllogistic exhibitions. Does Newman have to paraphrase the aesthetician here and say "De Principiis Non Disputandum Est?"[12] This is a question I shall be devoting a great deal of attention to below. But this much at least is clear. However else conflicts about first principles may be resolved, they will not be resolved by the use of formal inference alone.

> We are not able to prove by syllogism that there
> are any self-evident propositions at all; but
> supposing there are (as of course I hold there
> are), still who can determine these by logic?
> Syllogism, then, though of course it has its
> use, still does only the minutest and easiest
> part of the work, in the investigation of truth.
> For when there is any difficulty, that diffic-
> ulty commonly lies in determining first prin-
> ciples, not in the arrangement of proofs.[13]

Newman is aware that the limitations he places on the use of formal inference will suggest to many that he allows no legitimate place for it in human endeavours and, to the extent that logicality is equated with rationality, he will be deemed to be irrational. To prevent this misunderstanding, Newman waxes eloquent on the positive aspects of formal inference. He makes the following points:

1. Formal inference is the great principle of harmony in our thinking

    1. It reduces chaos to harmony

    2. It catalogues the accumulation of know-ledge

    3. It maps out the relation of the several departments of knowledge to each other

4. It is capable of correcting its own mis-
    takes.

2. Formal inference allows several intellects to
    bear on the same subject matter.

3. It shows us the direction in which truth lies,
    and how propositions lie toward one another
    (though not attaining to truth itself). It is
    a principal way in which discoveries are made
    though it does not in itself discover the un-
    known.

4. It indicates probabilities and improbabil-
    ities.

5. It suggests what is needed for proof.

6. It points out what is wanted in a theory, how
    a theory hangs together and what consequences
    flow from the theory.

7. It indicates where experience and observation
    should be applied, or where testimony should
    be sought for.

8. It holds facts together, explains difficulties, and reconciles the imagination to what
   is strange.[14]

But it belittles formal inference to treat it as a
mere organon. Like Moliere's Monsieur Jourdain "We
think in logic, as we talk in prose, without aiming at
doing so."[15] We instinctively put our conclusions into
words, as far as we are capable of so doing, for two
reasons; to satisfy ourselves and to justify ourselves
to others. Although such a verbal account of our reasoning cannot capture its full depth and extent, yet it
gives to what we hold a certain luminousness and force.

Inference is primarily concerned with notions. It
doesn't deal with things except indirectly. In concrete matters, abstract arguments can only approximate
to a proof. Since they cannot grasp the particular
they can only attain to probability, not to demonstration. "Science, working by itself, reaches truth
in the abstract, and probability in the concrete; but
what we aim at is truth in the concrete."[16] Science is
too simple and exact to be the measure of fact. As it
attains to perfection in its own sphere, for that very

reason it loses touch with particulars. Formal inference is wanting in two respects; its chain of premisses doesn't attain to first principles, and its chain
of conclusions doesn't attain to the concrete. The
first of these deficiencies has been considered in the
preceding section. Now we have to consider the second.
To establish Newman's point here I shall cite the long
footnote from the end of the section on formal inference in the Grammar.

> I have assumed throughout this Section that all
> verbal argumentation is ultimately syllogistic;
> and in consequence that it ever requires univer-
> sal propositions and comes short of concrete
> fact. A friend refers me to the dispute between
> Des Cartes and Gassendi, the latter maintaining
> against the former that "Cogito ergo sum" im-
> plies the universal "All who think exist." I
> should deny this with Des Cartes; but I should
> say (as indeed he said), that his dictum was not
> an argument but was the expression of a ratio-
> cinative instinct, as I explain below under the
> head of "Natural Logic."

> As to the instance "Brutes are not men;
> therefore men are not brutes," there seems to me
> no consequence here, neither a praeter nor a
> propter, but a tautology. And as to "It was
> either Tom or Dick that did it; it was not
> Dick, ergo," this may be referred to the one
> great principle on which all logical reasoning
> is founded, but really it ought not to be ac-
> counted an inference any more than if I broke a
> biscuit, flung half away, and then said of the
> other half, "This is what remains." It does but
> state a fact. So, when the 1st, 2nd, or 3rd
> proposition of Euclid II, is put before the eyes
> in a diagram, a boy, before he yet has learned
> to reason, sees with his eyes the fact of the
> thesis, and this seeing it even makes it diffi-

cult for him to master the mathematical proof. Here, then, a _fact_ is stated in the form of an argument.[17]

Formal inference is necessarily abstract because it makes essential use of generalizations and in so doing it fails to attain to the concrete fact.[18]

To what extent is Newman´s treatment of formal inference important? In one sense it is vital, for it clearly shows Newman to be no irrationalist, an accusation which has often been levelled against him. It should be clear from the foregoing discussion of formal inference that although Newman does not allow formal inference to be the whole of inference it does not follow that he allowed it no place at all. In another sense, Newman´s treatment of formal inference is not that important, for his primary concern in the _Grammar_ was to delineate that mode of reasoning which he called informal inference. To this subject we now turn.

Informal Inference

Newman has established that formal inference is not the method by which we attain to certainty in the concrete. What then is the real and necessary method?

It is the cumulation of probabilities, independent of each other, arising out of the nature
and circumstances of the particular case which
is under review; probabilities too fine to
avail separately, too subtle and circuitous to
be convertible into syllogisms, too numerous and
various for such conversion, even were they
convertible.[19]

Let us look more closely at each of the elements in

this description. The real and necessary method of

achieving certainty, Newman says, is the cumulation of

probabilities. It might be thought that what Newman

has in mind here is a simple numerical or additive not-

ion of cumulation, i.e. given the occurence of a suf-

ficient number of particular events...etc., the occur-

ence of another event is increased by the sum of the

probabilities of the particular event. But it is clear

from other parts of the Grammar that a merely numerical

concept of cumulation is insufficient. If I might be

permitted a mathematical analogy (since Newman himself

was so partial to them) then I should say that we are

not dealing with mere quantity but with vectors. It is

not sufficient simply to have a certain number of pro-

babilities; it is also necessary that these probabil-

ities be mutually supportive and that they form a co-

herent structure. It is this idea of structure, some

coherent unified whole of separate probabilities, that

enables Newman to escape what might be called the
"ten-leaky-buckets" objection. The idea here is that
if each of ten buckets fails to hold water, then the
entire collection of buckets will fail to hold water.
This may be true of buckets but as applied to the notion of informal inference the analogy is misleading.
Better is Newman's example of the cable, woven from
individual strands, no one of which can bear the weight
that the cable itself can bear.

The probabilities in informal inference are too
fine to avail separately. No one strand of reasoning
is sufficient to bear the entire weight of the inference. Since the probabilities are independent of each
other their mutually supportive interrelationship is
all the more striking. The probabilities arise out of
the nature of the case and are inescapably related to a
particular subject matter.

The probabilities are "too subtle and circuituous
to be convertible into syllogisms." They cannot, in
principle, be made into syllogisms, or put into syllogistic form. The probabilities are "too numerous and
various" to be convertible: that is, they are incapable, in fact, of being put into syllogistic form.

Klubertanz is one of those who recognizes clearly that

> [I]nformal inference is not simply an implicit, imperfect, inchoative formal inference. Newman, in fact, is convinced from his studies that the two kinds of inference are irreducible and have two different functions....It is further to be noted that informal inference cannot be <u>turned into</u> formal inference; the informal inference cannot become a formal one.[20]

A.J. Boekraad makes a similar point:

> Informal inference may be described as the combination of both natural and formal inferences. This, of course, has not to be taken as a formal juxtaposition of the two processes. It is rather the natural inference, which is of an implicit kind, partly worked out in explicit form, which we have found in formal inference. In natural inference, the human mind works simply spontaneously, "instinctively", as we have seen; in informal inference the mind has to make various of its media explicit.[21]

Boekraad is making essentially the same point I have been making in regard to the degrees of consciousness attached to the different kinds of inference. However, he then adds "these media will also be formal arguments of varying argumentative strength." If Boekraad is rehearsing Newman´s point that informal inference is continuous with formal inference, i.e. that the two kinds of inference can be connected in an actual chain of reasoning, then I have no dispute with him. If he means that formal inference is a constituent part of informal inference then his claim is clearly false.

Not everyone agrees that informal inference is logically independent of formal inference. Jay Newman[22] thinks that many of the inferences Newman regards as ´informal´ can be set out formally. The factory-girl argument is a case in point.

> "I think," says the poor dying factory-girl in the tale, "if this should be the end of all, and if all I have been born for is just to work my heart and life away, and to sicken in this dree place, with those mill-stones in my ears for ever, until I could scream out for t hem to stop and let me have a little piece of quiet, and with the fluff filling my lungs, until I thirst to death for one long deep breath of the clear air, and my mother gone, and I never able to tell her again how I loved her, and of all my troubles, --I think, if this life is the end, and that there is no God to wipe away all tears from all eyes, I could go mad!"

> Here is an argument for the immortality of the soul. As to its force, be it great or small, will it make a figure in a logical disputation, carried on <u>secundum</u> <u>artem</u>? Can any scientific common measure compel the intellects of Dives and Lazarus to take the same estimate of it? Is there any test of the validity of it better than the <u>ipse</u> <u>dixit</u> of private judgment, that is, the judgment of those who have a right to judge, and next, the agreement of many private judgments in one and view of it?[23]

Jay Newman offers us two arguments which, he claims, lack the spirit of the factory-girl´s actual reflections but contain essentially the same reasoning. Here is his reconstruction of the argument:

I

1. Goodness is not always rewarded in this life

2. Goodness must ultimately be rewarded

3. Therefore, the soul must be immortal.

II

1. There must be a source of perfect or absolute love, and perfect or absolute justice

2. Only God can provide perfect love or justice

3. Therefore, God exists.

It is Jay Newman's contention that arguments I and II embody the same rational content as the factory-girl's emotional outburst, without its rhetorical setting.

> To the extent that the Factory-Girl is offering us an argument, she is offering something which is no less "formal" than any other argument. The Factory-girl's argument - or arguments - may be, and ultimately must be, separated from the concrete setting of her remarks.[24]

It is ironic that Jay Newman controverts Newman on the nature of argument, not by arguing for his own position, but by asserting it. His view of reasoning might be dubbed the "monolithic theory" and it runs as follows. There is only one genus of argument. If the Factory Girl is offering us an argument it must belong to this genus, otherwise it is no real argument. Since all arguments are of the same kind, it follows that their concrete setting must be a matter of rhetorical decoration, the discarding of which will aid in a true appreciation of their logical worth.

It is difficult to know where to begin to reply to this controversion of one of Newman's basic theses. Fortunately, since Jay Newman does not argue for his claim but simply asserts it, it is not incumbent upon us to reply. It might be conceded that the Factory-Girl case is not as perspicuous an example of informal inference as might be desired. But all that this goes to show is that Jay Newman has picked a bad example. Many clear examples of informal inferences can be found in the Grammar which are incapable of being reconstituted as formal inferences.

The informal method of reasoning has three characteristics:[25]

1. It doesn't supersede formal inference

2. It is implicit

3. It is conditional.

First, informal inference, far from superseding formal inference, is one and the same with it. Newman's example of the attempt to convert the Protestant to Catholicism by means of a 'smart syllogism' was, presumably, meant to illustrate this point. This example is also meant to give some idea of the complexity of the real, substantial argument of which the syllogism is, as it were, merely the tip. The syllogism goes as follows:

Major premiss: All Protestants are bound to join the Church;

Minor Premiss: You are a Protestant;

Conclusion: You are bound to join the Church.

Here are some of the factors which have to be considered when considering the major premiss in this argument:

1. Are all Protestants bound to join the Church?

2. Are they so bound if they do not feel themselves bound?

3. Are they so bound if they feel their present religion is a safe one?

4. Are they so bound if they have grave doubts about the doctrinal purity and fidelity of the Church? Are they so bound if they are convinced that the Church is corrupt?

5. Are they so bound if their consciences instinctively reject certain of its doctrines?

6. Are they so bound if a study of history convinces them that the Pope's power is not <u>jure divino?</u>

The foregoing points might be considered anti-major; here are some pro-major points.

1. Can one believe Protestantism to be of divine origin?

2. Is all of Protestantism of divine origin?

3. If not, which parts are of divine origin?

4. Have not all the divine portions been, in fact, derived from the Church?

5. Did not the Church exist before Protestantism?

6. Can a Protestant be sure that Catholicism is not from above?

Some more general considerations pertinent to a resolution of the value of the major premiss in the syllogism are

1. What is a corruption?

2. What are the tests of corruption?

3. What is a religion?

4. Is it obligatory to profess any particular religion?.

5. What are the standards of truth and falsehood in religion?

So much for the major premiss;   What of the minor?
Here are some anti-minor points:

1.   I am not a Protestant

2.   I am a Catholic of the early undivided church

3.   I am a Catholic but not a Papist.

Some general considerations to be kept in mind in coming to a decision about the minor premiss of the syllogism are

1.   What is the value of unity in the Church?

2.   Is schism ever allowable?

3.   What is the weight of the Church's claim
     vis-a-vis personal judgement and responsibil-
     ity?

4.   Can we distinguish between the soul and the
     body of the Church?

5.   How is an obligation to change my religion to
     be weighed against prudential considerations?

6. Can I be sure of my sincerity of purpose in following the Divine will?

7. Have I the intellectual capacity to investigate these questions at all?

The general picture Newman has in mind here is this. Every formal inference has premisses which are themselves either the product of another formal inference, or the product of an informal inference. Formal inference and informal inference are thus complementary. If we wish to picture this scheme to ourselves we can conjure up the image of a tree with irregular branching. The bottom of the tree is the conclusion of the formal inference. The first bifurcation leads to the premisses of this inference. These are either themselves the product of another formal inference or the product of an informal inference. If they are the product of another formal inference we continue the ascent and eventually we will arrive at premisses which are the product of an informal inference.

Informal inference is implicit since it operates without "the direct and full advertence of the mind."[26] ´Instinct´ is the term Newman uses to describe this quasi-unconscious mode of operation.[27] The mind cannot completely analyse the motives carrying it to a certain conclusion. It is "determined by a body of proof, which it recognizes only as a body, and not in its constituent parts."[28]

However, informal inference and formal inference have at least one thing in common. They are both conditional. The conclusion of an inference, whether formal or informal, remains essentially dependent on its premisses. The conditionality of an informal inference is more problematic than that of a formal inference since the premisses of an informal inference, unlike those of a formal inference are implicit and vary in number and in estimated value according to whoever entertains them. In addition, Newman roundly asserts the relativity of proof to persons. "What to one intellect is a proof is not so to another."[29] This assertion is made, however, without prejudice to the objective truth or falsity of premisses.[30]

Newman gives us three examples to show how certitude results from arguments which, when taken in the letter, are but probabilities. The first, and most famous example, concerns the insularity of Great Britain.[31] We are certain, Newman notes, that Great Britain is an island. We have not a doubt in the world about it. Yet if we pause to consider the grounds on which we hold this belief, we see that they are far from forming a base from which this belief can be demonstratively derived. What kinds of factors can we point to support our belief? All that is available to us is such items as these:

1. We have been taught that Great Britain is an island since childhood

2. It is so on all the maps

3. This belief of ours has never been contradicted and is taken for granted by people, books, etc.

4. History, current events, the social and commercial systems, all these imply that Great Britain is an island.

In short, numerous facts rest on the truth of our belief, and no received opinion rests on its falsity.

Plainly, such considerations are not demonstrative. They are not such as to rule out hyperbolical
doubt. An unfriendly interlocutor could pose the following questions:

1. Have we circumnavigated Great Britain?

2. Do we know anyone who has?

3. Concerning the common belief that Great Britain is an island, how do we know that we are
   not simply taking the belief on each other's
   credit, somewhat in the fashion in which the
   legendary islanders made a living by taking in
   each other's washing?.

4. Is our general impression any more warranted
   that the once commonly held general impression
   that the world was flat?

Although we have no adamantine reply to these objections yet this does not disturb our certitude in the
least. We are sure of our conclusion without any doubt
and not in proportion to the evidence or on the balance
of the argument.

Newman's two other examples (the Case of the Latin Forgeries and the Inevitability of Death)[32] serve to reiterate the general form of the argument. In each case we have, as Newman, paraphrasing Locke, puts it, "a considerable surplusage...of belief over proof."[33]

Most of our most obstinate and reasonable certitudes are dependent on informal and personal proofs, which baffle analysis and cannot be brought under rule. According to Newman, this correlation between certitude and implicit proof is a law of our mind. For example, just as we normally see sense objects as a whole and do not construct them from a mass of detail, so too we grasp the legitimate conclusion of a concrete proof in and through the premisses. In concrete reasoning we relapse into that condition from which logic proposed to rescue us. We judge by ourselves, by our own lights, and on our own principles. Very often, our criterion of truth is not so much the manipulation of propositions as the intellectual and moral character of the person maintaining them.

Verbal argument (by which Newman means formal inference) is useful only in subordination to a higher logic (by which Newman means either informal inference or natural inference.) There follow several illustrations of this dictum. I shall mention only one.

Suppose we make the following claim: "There will be a European war for Greece is audaciously defying Turkey." How is the connective in this claim to be supported? Is it supported by a syllogism such as

1. All audacious defiances of Turkey on the part of Greece must end in a European war

2. This is a case of Greece audaciously defying Turkey

3. Therefore, we will have a European war.

Surely not! As Newman remarks, to support the connective in our original claim by appealing to this syllogism would be to explain the obscure by the more obscure. In fact, we determine the weight of the ´for´ by our knowledge of the particular circumstances of the Greece/Turkey situation, by appeal to uncatalogued experience, (our own or another´s), and by felt, rather than spoken, reflections. In practice, syllogism has no part in our assessment of the original claim. Here, then, we have a clear example of a proposition which, while it might itself constitute a premiss in a formal

inference, is, nevertheless, not in its turn the pro-

duct of a formal inference.

> [M]ethodical processes of inference, useful as
> they are, as far as they go, are only instru-
> ments of the mind, and need, in order to their
> due exercise, that real ratiocination and pre-
> sent imagination which gives them a sense beyond
> their letter, and which, while acting through
> them, reaches to conclusions beyond and above
> them. Such a living <u>organon</u> is a personal gift,
> and not a mere method or calculus.[34]

Most men (including Locke) agree that we often

have evidence enough for assent and certitude where

that evidence is not sufficient to support a scientific

proof.[35] Locke believes we can be certain of very few

propositions, Newman believes we can be certain of

many. Locke believes such certain propositions can be

recognized easily by common sense: Newman's view is

that the supra-logical judgement, which is our warrant

for certitude, is not mere commonsense but "the true

healthy action of our ratiocinative powers."[36] This

supra-logical judgement is both practical and specul-

ative. It does not operate by excluding formal infer-

ence but by complementing it. This judgement, which is

not part of our common nature but a personal gift, en-

sures that all proofs, except abstract demonstration,

have an element of the personal in them. We come to concrete conclusions, not by a mechanical necessity, but by the action of our minds operating conscientiously under a sense of duty to the conclusions.

Using the term ´moral´ to describe the type of certitude available to us in moral and spiritual matters, Newman goes on to insist that such ´moral´ certitude is all that is attainable in terrestrial and cosmic matters also. For example, take the matter of the earth´s rotation about the sun.

1. There is no formal demonstration of this.

2. There is a cluster of reasons, on different principles, which signify cumulatively.

3. This cluster amounts to a proof.

4. The mind is satisfied with what "amounts to a proof."

Newman asks us to compare this matter of the earth´s rotation with the proof of Revelation, as presented by Bishop Butler.[37] In this case also we have

1. no demonstration of the conclusion

2. cumulating and converging indicators

3. an indirect proof (<u>reductio</u> <u>ad</u> <u>absurdum</u>) of
    the conclusion

4. a feeling of mental repose.

According to Newman, there is one element which is
found in the theological case that is not found in the
astronomical one: the parties to the dispute must be
in a certain moral state, namely, they must be in earnest about religion and they must be capable of being
convinced on real evidence.[38]

Newman now asks himself a very important question.

> [G]ranting that the personality, so to speak, of
> the parties reasoning is an important element in
> proving propositions in a concrete matter, [can]
> any account...be given of the ratiocinative met-
> hod in such proofs over and above that analysis
> into syllogisms which is possible in each of its
> steps in detail?[39]

Newman´s answer, not surprisingly, is - Yes. The manner of his answer is, characteristically, indirect.

> [T]he principle of concrete reasoning is
> parallel to the method of proof which is the
> foundation of modern mathematical science....We
> know that a regular polygon, inscribed in a
> circle, its sides being continually diminished,
> tends to become that circle, as its limit; but
> it vanishes before it has coincided with the

circle, so that its tendency to be the circle,
though ever nearer fulfillment, never in fact
gets beyond a tendency. In like manner, the
conclusion in a real or concrete question is
foreseen and predicted rather than actually attained; foreseen in the number and direction of
accumulated premisses, which all converge to it,
and as the result of their combination, approach
it more nearly than any assignable difference,
yet do not touch it logically (though only not
touching it,) on account of the nature of its
subject-matter, and the delicate and implicit
character of at least part of the reasonings on
which it depends. It is by the strength, variety, or multiplicity of premisses which are are
only probable...by objections overcome, by adverse theories neutralized, by difficulties
gradually clearing up, by exceptions proving the
rule, by unlooked-for correlations found with
received truths, by suspense and delay in the
process issuing in triumphant reactions - by all
these ways and many others, it is that the practised and experienced mind is able to make a
sure divination that a conclusion is inevitable,
of which his lines of reasoning do not actually
put him in possession. This is what is meant by
a proposition being "as good as proved", a
conclusion as undeniable "as if it were proved,"
and by the reasons for it "amounting to a
proof", for a proof is the limit of converging
probabilities.[40]

Let us look at the elements of this account.

1. The conclusion is foreseen and predicted rat-

    her than actually attained:

            * in the number of accumulated premisses

            * in the direction of accumulated

              premisses

            * in the convergence/combination of

premisses.[41]

2. The conclusion is not actually obtained logic-
    ally because

    * the subject matter is always
      recalcitrant

    * the reasoning is implicit

3. The practised and experienced mind is enabled
    to be sure of its conclusions

    * by the strength of the individual
      premisses

    * by the variety of the individual
      premisses

    * by the multiplicity of the individual
      premisses

    * by objections overcome

    * by adverse theories neutralized

    * by gradual clearing up of difficulties

    * by unsought for correlations with
      received truth.

Newman notes that the logical form of this sort of
proof is indirect, a kind of _reductio ad absurdum_. It
differs from a real _reductio_ in that the premisses do

not actually 'touch' the conclusion, logically speaking. Newman is not saying that the process is illogical, merely that it is not logical in the sense of being demonstrative. In a key analogy, Newman likens the manner of proof in informal inference to the mathematical manner of determining the limit of a function or, in the citation just given, to the approach of a regular polygon with an ever-increasing number of sides to a circle. In the graphic representation of this phenomenon, the function approaches its limit asymtotically without ever actually reaching it.[42]

Having described the character of concrete reasoning Newman goes on to consider examples of it in which the reasoner admits to doing so in the way Newman has described.

In the first example, the physicist Wood, in discussing the character of the laws of motion, notes that they are not self-evident and that they do not admit of accurate proof. Yet on the other hand, they are constantly suggested to our senses, they agree with experiments as far as experiments can go, and the conclusions deduced from them are consistent with each other and with experimental results. Wood concludes that we can repose confidence in the truth of the laws of motion.

Newman notes that Wood's conclusion is not proved but "is as good as proved." We would be irrational to deny it to be virtually proved since the deficiencies in the proof arise from natural facts and, insofar as these can be corrected, the case approximates to a proof. Further, when the laws are assumed as hypotheses, light is shed on a multitude of collateral facts.

The other two examples which Newman gives possess similar features. In each case, the conclusion is, logically speaking, out of sight; we can make a reasonable judgement that the conclusion is as good as proved even though admitting of no logical argument; and in each case, the various details are more or less implicit and impalpable.

Newman's thought on informal inference was the product of years of reflection. In an unpublished paper from the year 1853 entitled "On the Certainty of Faith" he makes the distinction between formal inference and informal inference in terms of 'seeing' and

´feeling´ propositions to be true, and also in terms of Evidentia Veritatis and Evidentia Credibilitatis.[43] This treatment of the topic from another angle helps us see clearly just what Newman was up to.

When we see a proposition to be true, says Newman, we say that it is clear, or that it is surrounded with a certain light, which theologians call ´evidentia.´ If we now drop metaphors and say plainly what this seeing, this clearness or evidentia is, we shall say that by ´evidentia´ is meant the witness of existing or ascertained truths to a certain further proposition that it is their correlative, or hangs together with them.

This account of ´evidentia´ differs somewhat from the account of formal inference in the Grammar. Here, the relationship that exists between the ´evidentia´ and the proposition for which it is the ´evidentia´ is a relationship of logical consistency rather than a relationship of logical implication. And since logical consistency, while a necessary condition of logical implication, is not equivalent to it, it is evident that Newman´s thought underwent some development on this matter between 1853 and 1870. In the Grammar consistency is the mark of informal inference rather than the mark of formal inference, while strict logical implication is reserved to the domain of the latter. Let there be nine true propositions and let there be a tenth which just completes or fits into them, then this tenth is true also because it and none but it fits.[44] We feel a proposition to be true when, though we cannot see that it fits or snaps into existing recognised truths, yet we have reason for anticipating that, did we know those other existing truths more fully, we should see they presupposed or required it. Truths that we _see_ fall under the category of necessary matter and are syllogized, or have logical proof. Truths that we _feel_ are in contingent matter and are gained not by syllogism but by induction, i.e. not by one simple and sufficient proof but by a complex argument consisting of accumulating and converging probabilities. We do not have a strict logical proof of the proposition "all men die" but we do have cumulating and converging reasons for assenting to that proposition.[45]

What is _evidentia_ to one man may not be _evidentia_ to another: (a) the principles, existing truths, or premisses of one discipline are not the same as that of another, and (b) one set of existing truths or premisses may be easier of apprehension to the human mind than another.[46] Principles at first difficult and therefore recondite become easier the more they are dwelt on and tried. In difficult and recondite subject matters those who have studied them are more likely to attain the conclusion which these premisses exhibit. Scientific proof is not merely logical proof, but logical proof from generally ascertained and received principles. This is the key to the distinction between Evidentia Veritatis and Evidentia Credibilitatis. Evidentia Credibilitatis differs from Evidentia Veritatis in this: it proves the truth apprehended, not true, but credible, or really true. It proves its credibility not by any scientific process resting on generally received principles and drawn out in exact syllogisms, but by the action of the individual mind, which knows what others may or may not know, and acts, not necessarily by rule, but by practical expertness.

Newman gives the following example. Let us suppose that we are considering a historical question of whether a certain writer was the author of an anonymous book. As is often the case there are reasons which support both sides of the case. The reasons against his being the author are:

1. It is not likely he should have time to write it.

2. It is not likely he should have the will to write it.

3. It is not likely that he should have the power to write it.

The reasons in favour of the proposition that he did write the book are:

1. It is commonly ascribed to him.

2. It is ascribed to no one else.

3. He has not denied it as he did of another volume in a former case.

4. Very few but he could have written it, from the necessary position of the author, whoever he is.

5. There are many things in it like his writing.

6. The closer it is examined, the more things are to be found in it in favour of his being the author.

7. The better his writings are known, the more this book will seem like his, etc., etc. (23)

Your opponent on this question will very likely dispute your probabilities. How then are you to sustain them? For example, take the fourth point in favour of the thesis, "Very few but he could have written it". Your opponent would be forced to admit it, could you but give him all your grounds for holding it. But this is the rub. This is precisely Newman's point. One probability branches out into another and so on, for practical purposes, ad infinitum. So, in matters of this kind, you cannot then prove your point to another. In fact, the argument given above is not a proof in the strict sense. At most, it is like a proof; it comes short of a proof in fact.

It is clear from all the above that Newman's thought on what came to be called informal inference was more or less fixed in its essentials as early as

1853. On the other hand, his thought on what came to be called formal inference underwent some development and refinement until it found full expression in the Grammar.

Natural Inference

The exercise of reason in its natural state can profitably be compared to the exercise of sense or memory. Just as we do not ordinarily know how we sense or how we remember, so too, we are not aware of the route we take in passing from antecedent to consequent in a piece of ratiocination nor, indeed, are we aware of the antecedents themselves. The analogy between the operation of sense and natural inference is throughgoing. For, as we do not know how we sense, so too, in natural inference, we are not aware of the route from antecedent to consequent. And as in sensing, the _terminus a quo_ is a material object and not a proposition, so too, in natural inference, the _terminus a quo_ is an experienced state of affairs which is not expressed propositionally. Newman here gives us the first intimation that natural inference differs from both formal

inference and informal inference in a significant respect. Both formal inference and informal inference
have actual propositions as their termini a quo and
even in informal inference there is a partial awareness
of the connection between the premisses and the
conclusion. Natural reasoning, on the other hand, is
apprehended by us as a simple indivisible act. Newman
calls the move in natural inference from antecendent to
consequent ´instinctive´ meaning by this that it is
spontaneous and inevitable.[47] Our natural mode of reasoning has another peculiarity in that it is not a move
from proposition to proposition but rather a move from
things to things, from wholes to wholes, from concrete
to concrete. "To the mind itself the reasoning is a
simple divination or prediction."[48] We find this mode
of reasoning especially (though not exclusively) exemplified in two classes of people: the foolish, who
know nothing of the intellectual arts, and the wise,
who don´t need them. While everyone possesses this
capacity for natural reasoning to some degree, in ordinary minds it is biased and degraded by prejudice,
passion and self-interest. However, in a few cases it
is characterised by subtlety and truth. Newman gives
us two examples to illustrate his point. The first

example is that of the uneducated weather-wise peasant, manifestly one of those who knows nothing of the intellectual arts. The second example is that of the expert diagnostician who is one of those who does not need the intellectual arts. Let us look at what Newman says about the weather-wise peasant:

> A peasant who is weather-wise may yet be simply unable to assign intelligible reasons why he thinks it will be fine tomorrow; and if he attempts to do so, he may give reasons wide of the mark; but that will not weaken his own confidence in his prediction. His mind does not proceed step by step, but he feels all at once and together the force of various combined phenomena, though he is not conscious of them.[49]

(I shall have more to say about this example shortly.) The expert diagnostician is in much the same case except that he operates on a higher intellectual level. There is still, however, the same inability to give satisfactory reasons, the same unconscious apprehension of multifarious and recondite phenomena, and the same accuracy in prediction.

This natural faculty of ratiocination can, at times, rise to the level of genius. Newman takes as an example Isaac Newton whose perception of mathematical and physical truth was far in advance of his ability to give proofs for these truths.[50]

We can gain some further insight into this faculty
of natural reasoning by comparing it to taste. Both
natural reasoning and taste are exercised spontaneously
once acquired. Both are inarticulate in their modes of
procedure. Neither of them goes by rule though both of
them admit of analysis. Newman denies that natural
inference is a general capacity. It is, rather, attached to a specific subject-matter depending on the
individual in question. As against Aristotle, he holds
that reasoning, in the broad sense of the term, is not
primarily an instrumental art: as against Dr.
Johnson, he holds that reasoning is not a general capacity. In fact Newman goes so far as to claim that the
reasoning faculty is not so much one faculty as a collection of similar faculties assembled under one name.
Analogously, memory is operative for us in particular
departments and functions better in some than in
others.

Newman concludes the section with a striking passage on the importance of the personal element in natural inference.

> Instead of trusting logical science, we must
> trust persons, namely, those who by long ac-
> quaintance with their subject have a right to
> judge. And if we wish ourselves to share in
> their convictions and the ground of them, we

must follow their history, and learn as they
have learned. We must take up their particular
subject as they took it up, beginning at the
beginning, give ourselves to it, depend on practice and experience more than on reasoning, and
thus gain that mental insight into truth, whatever its subject-matter may be, which our mas-
ters have gained before us. By following this
course, we may make ourselves of their
number...directing ourselves by our own moral or
intellectual judgment, not by our skill in argumentation.[51]

Let us examine Newman's example of the meteoroso-

phical peasant. If the process described in the pas-

sage is really one of inference then the phenomena men-

tioned must at least be capable (in principle) of being

expressed propositionally (at least to some extent),

i.e. they must be proponible. In this example, then,

the peasant is not conscious of the premisses of the

inference, qua premisses, though he is, necessarily,

conscious of the phenomenal ground these premisses

would have if they were expressed propositionally. The

peasant's apprehension of the grounds of these propon-

ible premisses is global and undifferentiated. In my

opinion, this is what Newman means by claiming that the

peasant feels the force of the various combined phen-

omena though he is not conscious of them. Given his

unconsciousness of the premisses, it' follows, of course, that the peasant can hardly be aware of their interconnections and their relationship to the conclusion. It is this unconsciousness of both the premisses and their relationship to the conclusion that leads Newman to say that natural inference is 'instinctive' and that it appears to be "a simple divination or prediction."[52] If we are like the peasant, we experience the phenomena and derive the conclusion, all without any consciousness of premisses or their relation to the conclusion.

Insofar as there is a real inability (in principle) to express the experienced phenomena, it seems to me that the putative inference is no inference at all and that the so-called 'conclusion' of the inference is merely the propositional expression of a certain range of experience. My contention is that if there really is an inference here, then its grounds must be proponible. If this is not the case and it is impossible, in principle, to express these grounds propositionally, then what we have is not an inference but rather an intuition (i.e. the seeing x to be a base-level x) or an interpretation of our experience.

In his example, Newman notes that the peasant _feels_ the force of the various phenomena (so there _are_ grounds) but is not conscious of them. What does it mean to be able to _feel_ something without being conscious of it? It seems that to _feel_, in this context, is simply to be aware _that_ forces are moving us towards a conclusion (awareness-that) while to be conscious is to be aware, in addition to the foregoing, of _what_ these forces are (awareness-what.) It may be that pure cases of awareness-that are not possible, that is, one could never have awareness-that without some degree of awareness-what.

It would seem that the peasant knows the kinds of factors that are relevant to his claim, namely, the colour of the sky, the lumbago in his back, etc. The factors are multifarious and belong to different orders so that the peasant´s consciousness of them is global and unfocussed. I am claiming that the word ´feel,´ in Newman´s example, is best interpreted as a global or undifferentiated consciousness rather than as a complete lack of consciousness altogether. If Newman intends to exclude rigorously every kind of awareness then it is difficult to see how his example remains one

of inference. He may, of course, call it ´natural in-
ference´ if he so wishes but then it must be distinguished from that natural inference which is the limiting case of informal inference. This pseudo-natural
inference is, as I have indicated above, really an intuition or base-level interpretation of our experience.
Natural inference proper is the limiting case of informal inference in terms of degrees of conscious mediation. In some ways it is a significantly different kind
of inference from either the formal or the informal
variety. Both formal inference and informal inference
move from actual proposition to actual proposition even
while they differ in the process by which they make
this move. In other ways, natural inference belongs
firmly in the camp of informal inference. In formal
inference the move from proposition to proposition is
logical; in informal inference the premisses do not
logically touch the conclusion at all! In the case of
natural inference, not only is the process unconscious
(which it also is to some extent in informal inference)
but it seems that the antecedents themselves are not
propositions but rather what I have called proponibles.
The terms Newman uses to describe natural inference
(simple indivisible act, instinct, divination, etc.)

indicate that what we have in natural inference is a proposition for which there may be phenomenal grounds but for which there is no evidence, i.e. no actual supporting propositions.[53] If natural inference is really to be inference there must be a minimal consciousness of these phenomenal grounds. Unless that minimal consciousness exists what we have is intuition rather than inference.

A problem which can arise is that both genuine cases of natural inference and what I have been calling intuition or interpretation can be characterized as a simple or indivisible act. In reality, the former merely appear to be that way because of the diffused consciousness of the premisses and their interconnections, while the latter really are simple and indivisible. In one crucial passage Newman seems to recognize the possibility that what he has been calling natural inference is not really inference at all. He has been talking about the ability of idiots savants to perform mathematical computation with accuracy and ease. Newman claims that these people do not reason by method but merely by instinct. He realizes that there are those who will insist that the idiots are really reasoning by method even if the method cannot be made explicit. Anticipating this objection, Newman says

> I do not think it matters for my purpose, whether we say that the logic is implicit, or that there is no real logic except as symbolical -- so that conscious analysis is not required as possessed by the unlearned etc.[54]

This seems to indicate that Newman's major concern was not so much to show natural inference to be inference as to show it to be unconscious.[55] Because both natural inference and intuition/interpretation are largely unconscious, there is a real danger of confusing the one with the other.[56]

If my interpretation is correct, then natural inference, qua inference, is merely the limiting case of informal inference. It differs from the paradigm instances of informal inference in that the process is completely unconscious rather than partially so. However, it is similar to informal inference in that it begins from what are in essence propositions even if it remains largely unaware of them. On the other hand, if Newman is serious in his claim about the complete non-consciousness of the phenomenal grounds of the inference then what he calls natural inference is not merely the limiting case of informal inference. While it too is unconscious, it is also the case that it does not begin from premisses, either expressed or unexpressed. This natural inference is really not inference at all. It is, rather, some kind of primitive or basic apprehension of a state of affairs and the propositional expresssion of that apprehended state of affairs. In short, it is, to use Newman's own terminology, an assent. In a passage in the Grammar, Newman says

> What is called reasoning is often only a peculiar and personal mode of abstraction, and so far, like memory, may be said to exist without antecedents. It is a power of looking at things in some particular aspect, and of determining their internal and external relations thereby.[57]

A little further on in the same passage, Newman explicitly uses the word 'interpretation' when describing the operation of this abstractive process.

> [In abstracting] we determine correctly or otherwise, as it may be; but in either case, it is by a sense proper to ourselves; for another may see the objects which we are thus using, and give them quite a different interpretation, inasmuch as he abstracts another set of general notions from those same phenomena which present themselves to us also.[58]

From the first passage it is not immediately clear whether Newman means that this abstraction is really a method of reasoning properly so called, or whether it is called reasoning but really is not so. I take him

to consider it to be a real form of reasoning for the
following reasons. I mentioned elsewhere that Newman,
in contradistinction to Whateley, considered generalization to be a form of inference. His exact words are

> I conceive that generalization is a sort of in-
> ference -- for it implies a conclusion about the
> similarity of the things generalized.[59]

This seems to show beyond any shadow of a doubt that
Newman wants to lump together as inference what I have
been distinguishing as natural inference proper and
intuition/interpretation. In my opinion, Newman is
just wrong here. We do not conclude concerning the
similarity of things generalized, we simply recognize
their similarity. Newman's example betrays his confusion:

> If I threw together Christian Sacraments, bene-
> dictions and relics, into one class with magical
> incantations, phylactaries, amulets, philtres,
> and horse shoes, under the common name of spell
> or charm, it would be an inference , and a false
> inference, but not a syllogism.[60]

Newman is right. This is not a syllogism. But neither
is it an inference, true or false! It is simply a
classification or an interpretation. Newman gives us
another example of an inference which is not a syllogism: "no Christians are bad men, therefore no bad men
are Christians."[61] What is of interest here is that

Newman, in the Grammar, denies that such a concatenation of sentences is an inference! Such seeming inferences are merely facts stated in the form of an argument.[62] Whether Newman is correct in so characterizing this particular example, it is of interest to note that Newman did not similarly characterize what I have been calling intuition/interpretation, but instead considered it to be a form of inference.

In discussing Newman on natural inference, Boekraad has this to say:

> As it is found in man he calls it [instinct] also intuition, that is, the drawing out of a general proposition "from our ever-recurring experiences of its testimony (namely, that of the external world) in particulars." This would seem to be very near to our notion of abstraction, yet it does not seem that the ordinary idea of abstraction covers Newman's meaning for he continues: "it is a force which spontaneously impels us, not only to bodily movements but to mental acts". (Grammar, pp. 61-62)[63]

Boekraad is right. Newman's use of the term ´instinct´ is very close to our notion of abstraction. To understand what is going on here let us look at the passage from which Boekraad derives his citation. I shall quote the entire passage without misgivings as it contains not only remarks on intuition and instinct, but also contains Newman's prime example of a first principle.

> Next, as to the proposition, that there are
> things existing external to ourselves, this I do
> consider a first principle, and one of universal
> reception. It is founded on an instinct; I so
> call it, because the brute creation possesses
> it. This instinct is directed towards individ-
> ual phenomena, one by one, and has nothing of
> the character of a generalization; and, since
> it exists in brutes, the gift of reason is not a
> condition of its existence, and it may justly be
> considered an instinct in man also. What the
> human mind does is what brutes cannot do, viz.
> to draw from our ever recurring experiences of
> its testimony in particulars a general propos-
> ition, and, because this instinct or intuition
> acts whenever the phenomena of sense present,
> themselves, to lay down in broad terms, by an
> inductive process, the great aphorism, that
> there is an external world, and that all the
> phenomena of sense proceed from it. This gener-
> al proposition, to which we go on to assent,
> goes...far beyond our experience...64

The first thing to note here is that this passage is

not contained on the section on "Natural Inference"!

It is found in the section on "Presumption", which is

where Newman first treats of first principles in any

detail in the Grammar. There is no reason to think

that Newman is talking about natural inference here at

all. What makes Boekraad think that Newman is discuss-

ing natural inference? Perhaps, the fact that he is

talking here about instinct, and that elsewhere he des-

cribes natural inference as being instinctive. But

from the fact that natural inference is instinctive it

does not follow that <u>only</u> natural inference is instinctive. As Newman's example clearly shows, what is going on here is not natural inference but what I have been calling instinct/intuition or what Boekraad, correctly, calls abstraction.

Given that Newman's primary distinction in the <u>Grammar</u> is between inference and assent and that his basic problem is how we are legitimately entitled to move from the former to the latter, it is surely significant that in his very setting out of the problem he should have overlooked this crucial ambiguity in his notion of natural inference.

Among Newman's numerous commentators only one has noticed this ambiguity. M.J. Ferreira notes that Newman's emphasis on natural inference's being altogether unconscious and implicit seems to make it the most basic form of informal inference, in terms of degrees of conscious mediation. Ferreira goes on to note that Newman writes of cases where not only is the medium unconscious but the antecedents also. He suggests that lack of consciousness of antecedents indicates that in this case natural inference is something other than the limiting case of informal inference.[65] He then raises

the question of whether natural inference is really
inference at all. Although attracted to the
"non-inference" view of natrual inference Ferreira finally decides against it. He gives the following reasons. First, Newman asserts that inference is a <u>sine</u>
<u>qua</u> <u>non</u> of assent. Second, Newman's claim that infor-
mal inference is one and the same with formal inference
might apply to natural inference as well. Third,
Newman's frequent references to the distinction between
having reasons and giving reasons suggests he saw the
necessity for some kind of justifying inference for all
assents. Ferreira concludes that most of the evidence
points to natural inference being really inference.

> Newman's few contrasting hints to the contrary
> may reveal the germ of a deeper insight into the
> way we reach conclusions...but an insight which
> he could not develop because of his commitment
> to the prevailing view of 'justified' belief.[66]

I agree with Ferreira's conclusion but I disagree
with his first and third reasons for holding it. I
agree with his second point which is that Newman's
claim that formal inference is one and the same with
informal inference applies to natural inference as
well. One of my claims throughout this chapter has
been that inference is a continuum, the limits of which

are formal inference and natural inference. Concerning
Ferreira's first point: inference is a sine qua non of
reflex or complex assent only, not of simple assent.
Ferreira fails to appreciate the incipient confusion
between natural inference proper and intuition and this
leads him to think that natural inference precedes simple assent as well as complex assent.[67] In the next
chapter I shall argue that simple assent is not preceded by natural inference but is, rather, an intuition.[68] Ferreira's third point rests on the same failure
to appreciate the possibility of confusion between natural inference proper and intuition.

The Argument From Conscience

Newman's argument from conscience to the existence
of God is often taken to be a paradigm example of an
informal inference.[69] My purpose in this final section
is to show that the argument from conscience cannot be
classed as either formal inference, informal inference,
or natural inference and so, in Newman's terms, cannot
be properly called an argument at all.[70]

Newman's actual line of argument in the Grammar is as follows.[71] An act of conscience, though one and indivisible, nevertheless has two clearly distinguishable aspects. Conscience may be considered as a moral sense, as a rule of right conduct to be followed here and now. This first aspect of conscience Newman terms 'critical.' Under this aspect, conscience is clearly fallible and variable. So, although a man must follow his own conscience he cannot rely on it unquestioningly as an impeccable guide. Newman's argument to God is not based on this aspect of conscience. The other aspect which we may discern in the act of conscience Newman terms 'judicial.' This is conscience as a sense of duty, as a magisterial dictate. It is on this aspect of conscience that Newman's argument to God is based. Under this aspect of conscience I become aware that I am submitted to a law higher than, and quite different from, any man-made law. Like taste, conscience is essentially a personal matter but, unlike taste, conscience has an intentional thrust. Whereas taste reposes in itself, conscience reaches forward to discern a sanction higher than self. When we consider conscience in its judicial or magisterial capacity we become painfully aware that it dictates and commands in a way that no man can dictate and command. Conscience relates us to something exterior and superior to the self. As yet, this could be merely a quasi-Kantian moral law, for the intentional quality of conscience merely indicates the existence of something whose nature is, as yet, unspecified. However, conscience also possesses other phenomenological features which flesh out the bare intentional entity so far disclosed. In our transgression of conscience we experience feelings of reverence, awe, fear, and remorse. These feelings are such that we feel them only in the presence of other people. Though these feelings have analogues in other situations, yet, as they occur specificially in the context of conscience they disclose the presence of a Person before whom I feel myself responsible and to whom my life belongs in some way.

Conscience, then, is a manifestation of a living contact between myself and God. In the experience of conscience (in its magisterial aspect) there is present to me a concrete, though partial, representation of the one Person who is solely Good. According to Newman, for real apprehension we must have recourse to an image. (This image does not necessarily have to be construed in crudely visual terms as H.H. Price and others suppose.) Conscience supplies us with an image of God in which he is made present to us under his attributes of justice and judgement.

Newman considers and refutes two objections to the foregoing line of argument. The first objection insists that Newman is putting the cart before the horse. We can recognize a law as a law, and as having binding force over us, only if we already know the law-giver and the fact of his promulgation of that law. We cannot, therefore, recognize conscience in its magisterial aspect unless we already know God to exist and conscience to be a manifestation of His commands. This objection derives whatever little force it has from the context of positive law. But conscience is revelatory of man's own nature and its necessity and its binding character can be apprehended without a prior apprehension of God as its author.

The second objection is based on the claim that the unbeliever simply doesn't experience the feelings that Newman claims are associated with conscience. Newman replies that it is not true that the unbeliever cannot experience the same feelings as the believer

though it is true, and even likely, that he will experience them to lesser degree and with less intensity.
These feelings are part of man's nature and are common
to all, though they may not be present in all to the
same degree. Newman is not making the claim that these
feelings are sufficient in themselves to disclose God's
presence, but he does want to insist that they can give
rise to trains of thought which will yield certitude to
a person who esteems moral values.

Finally, Newman is not making the claim that conscience is independent in all its manifestations, of
extrinsic factors. He recognizes the importance of
early training for the development of a well-trained
and informed conscience. Still, all that extrinsic
factors can provide is a modification of the original
faculty: they cannot bring about its creation.

This argument is clearly not a metaphysical argument. It is not intended, however, to replace metaphysical arguments but to supplement them. Neither is it
a variant of the moral argument[72] which can be compres-
sed and summarized in syllogistic form. Newman is not
arguing that a law implies a lawgiver but rather that
conscience manifests an absolute law which all men must

obey and that conscience is, as such, an image of the divine lawmaker. The argument is, rather, a way to God designed to impress the person who already believes in Him but doesn't know how to think of Him. It is not so much a way of discovering the unknown God as of vividly realizing (in Newman's terms, really assenting to) the living God.[73]

In the Grammar, Newman is not concerned with metaphysical arguments that are in principle open to any rational person willing to consider them. He is instead trying to convince the reader that he (Newman) has perfectly good reasons of his own for believing in God that others may find for themselves if they will but look elsewhere than to "Universal Reason." In concrete matters there is no justification for presuming that it is intrinsically possible to locate formalized demonstrations which will infallibly convince all open-minded men of the conclusions which they are supposed to establish. An argument will only succeed in being demonstrative to those people who find that its premisses harmonize with their basic first principles. Newman is reasoning from what he knows of his own conscience and its working and from what he knows of inter-personal relationships. He invites us to do likewise, and that invitation is the argument insofar as there is any argument here at all.

The argument as found in "Proof of Theism" is essentially the same save that there Newman locates it in the context of a rudimentary theory of mind.[74] One is conscious of one's existence but

> Consciousness indeed is not of simple being, but of action or passion, of which pain is one form. I am conscious that I am, because I am conscious that I am thinking (cogito ergo sum) or feeling, or remembering, or comparing, or (exercising) discourse.[75]

The fact that one's consciousness of one's existence is mediated through particular states or operations reveals to Newman an important principle:

> Sentio ergo sum. To call this an act of argumentation or deduction, and that it implies, faith in that reasoning process which is denoted by the symbol of (ergo) seems to me a fallacy." I do not advance from on e proposition to another, when I know (-am conscious-) my existence from being conscious of) my feeling but one and the same act of consciousness brings home to me that which afterwards at leisure I draw out into two propositions, denoting two out of the many aspects of the one thing. What is called reasoning then is in its essence not a deduction, but it is the perception of certain complex ideas, or the modes or the dress of things. Thought and being, or sensation & being, are brought home to me by one act of consciousness, prior to any exercise of ratiocination, though I may afterwards, if I wish, survey the complex idea by means of that exercise.[76]

Now it is clear from the foregoing that Newman denies that the ´ergo´ in ´Sentio ergo sum´ is expressive of any kind of formal inference. We have here no act of argument or deduction.[77] Newman, however, does not wish to exclude reasoning in every sense of the term. The key sentence in the passage is "What is called reasoning is in its essence not a deduction, but it is the perception of certain complex ideas." Here Newman expresses very clearly that fundamental conflation of reasoning with intuition which pervades both this paper and the Grammar. That Newman does indeed conflate these two distinct notions can be seen from this revealing passage:

> That one man sees what another does, that A & B are alike arises from no comparison & discrimination of outlines, complexion, feature etc. but it arises from the way in which he, (and not another perhaps) looks at them. It is a kind of intuition, and hence it is very difficult to separate what is called reasoning from intuition.[78]

It is indeed very difficult to separate reasoning from intuition and Newman fails to do so throughout this paper and, if I am correct, throughout the Grammar. Part of Newman´s difficulty arises from the fact that insofar as he wishes to use the word ´intuition´ at all he wishes to limit its use to the apprehension of inward states. He is reluctant to speak of an intuition in regard to extra-mental states.

> If I could I would make an arbitrary definition of intuition viz. that it referred to our <u>inter-nal</u> acts only. It exercises...itself on nothing external to us, as the being of God, the exis-tence of an external world etc, but it relates to our own mental operations.[79]

This will not do. For just as what is disclosed by conscience is the real, extra-mental existence of a Judge, so too, sensation discloses to us the existence of a real external world. The process of intuition is the same in both cases: modes of the mind, which are constitutive of consciousness, have permanent and re-curring features.[80] I cannot deny that Newman himself does not use the term 'intuition' here. Instead, he calls this process 'reasoning.' But, as he himself admits, it is difficult to separate reasoning from in-tuition.

This 'argument' from conscience is clearly not a formal inference. Neither is it an informal infer-ence.[81] If it is compared to the paradigmatic examples of informal inference examined above it will be seen to differ from them in some important respects, the most notable being the following. In informal inference, the premisses are not only many, they are also varied.

Moreover, the conclusion of an informal inference is not simply a statement of some property which is possessed in common by the phenomena but rather an enunciation of a proposition which is different in content from any of the supporting premisses. Now, in the case of the argument from conscience, the ´premisses´ are all acts of conscience and the ´conclusion´ is simply a proposition to the effect that all these acts possess some features in common.

Is the argument from conscience then a case of natural inference? To my mind, this is the only plausible category of inference under which it can be subsumed. However, as I have argued above, Newman has two distinct usages for the term ´Natural Inference.´ In the first use of the term, it signifies the limiting case of informal inference, differing from informal inference proper only in degree of conscious mediation. As the argument from conscience is not an informal inference, neither is it this kind of natural inference. Newman´s second use of the term ´natural inference´ is simply equivalent to intuition.

While intuition and natural inference are distinct, they are not unrelated. Intuition is a virtual component of natural inference. This is what I meant above when I insisted that the phenomenal basis of natural inference be proponible. In the case both of intuition and natural inference there is an apprehension of multifarious factors but in intuition, this apprehension is of one aspect and one aspect only and the intuitive proposition simply expresses the character of this one aspect. In natural inference it is otherwise. Here, a proposition is enunciated which is not simply the characterization of some repeated aspect of experience. It is a genuine conclusion based on (virtual) propositions, which propositions may be intuitions.

Take the case of the meteorosophical peasant. Here we have a genuine case of natural inference. The phenomena which the peasant experiences are such as: the sky's being red; the air pressure dropping; the sheep's being excessively skittish, etc. These are all very different kinds of experience. The peasant probably does not encapsulate these experiences in propositional form. His prognostication is, however, a proposition, and it differs from any of the virtual propositions which support it evidentially. In the case of the argument from conscience, what lies at its base is simply the apprehension of recurrent features of acts of conscience. Here, the experience is all of a kind. The ´conclusion´ of the argument is reached via a phenomenological analysis of these acts of conscience.

Newman´s argument from conscience is, then, no argument at all. It is not subsumable under any of the species of inference: formal, informal or natural. It is rather the articulation of the intuitively apprehended features of certain mental acts coeval with consciousness. Newman shares with us this articulation of the phenomenon of conscience and invites us to examine our own acts of conscience so that we may verify the accuracy of his articulation.[82]

Summary Conclusion

In this chapter, I have tried to give an account of Newman´s notion of inference. My claim is, that on a careful reading of the texts, the following facts emerge:

1. Formal, informal and natural inference form a continuum in terms of degrees of conscious mediation.

2. Formal inference is logically distinct from both informal and natural inference.

3. Informal inference and natural inference are distinct from one another only in terms of degrees of conscious mediation.

4. The term ´Natural Inference´ is used to signify two quite distinct acts of the mind: (1) a limiting case of informal inference, and (2) an intuition.

I have been primarily interested in becoming clear on what inference is in itself rather than on what it is in relation to other Newmanian notions. For this reason, I am delaying a critical consideration of the notion of ´conditionality´ until the third chapter.

Notes

[1]J.H. Newman, An Essay in Aid of a Grammar of Assent (Notre Dame, 1979). "Inference is conditional
because a conclusion at least implies the assumption of
premisses" (p. 28); "Inference is in its nature and by
its profession conditional and uncertain" (p. 65.);
"The latter [inference] is an acceptance on the condition of the acceptance of the premisses" (p. 76); "The
special characteristic of inference is that it is conditional" (p. 145); "Inference...holds propositions
conditionally" (p. 157); "Inference is the conditional
acceptance of a proposition" (p. 209); Subsequent
references to the Grammar of Assent will be abbreviated
thus: Grammar.

[2]Grammar, p. 209.

[3]This is all I shall have to say about natural
inference here. The third section of the present chapter contains a more detailed and sustained discussion.

[4]Grammar, p. 211.

[5]Grammar, p. 211.

[6]Grammar, pp. 211-212.

[7]Grammar, p. 212. Strictly speaking, this statement refers only to formal inference for, as we have
seen, natural inference is largely an unconscious process.

[8]As an example of such ambiguity, Newman instances
the word ´inference´ itself. This can mean
    *   the mental act of inferring
    *   the connecting principle, or inferentia,
        beteen premisses and conclusion
    *   the conclusion itself.

[9]The image that Newman uses to capture this process of emasculation is that of the "rivers, full,
winding, and beautiful" turned into navigable canals.
(215) Our aim in inference is, humpty-dumptyishly, to
have the words mean just what we choose them to mean.
Their innumerable natural implications and connotations
are to be eliminated or reduced as much as possible.

[10]Grammar, p. 216. It might be objected that even if the premisses of a given demonstration needed to be supported by still more premisses, this does not affect the demonstrative character of the inference under consideration. The response to this objection is simply that Newman is working with an Aristotelian notion of demonstration. At the foundation of Aristotelian demonstration we find 'primary premisses' or 'basic truths,' i.e. propositions which have no other propositions logically prior to them. The possibility of a regress of justification in regard to any putative demonstration is sufficient to show it to be no demonstration. See the fourth chapter for a brief discussion of the Aristotelian elements in Newman's thought.

[11]One could object that since first principles underlie all our inferences and since, ex hypothesi, first principles are 'primary premisses' or 'basic truths', that formal inference is, after all, demonstration. To put this objection forward is, however, to miss Newman's point, which is that, in concrete matters we do not have first principles at the immediate base of formal inferences. Rather, informal inference mediates between the proximate premisses of the formal inference and the first principles which constitute the ultimate foundation for all inferences. This is the point to Newman's remarks about the complementarity of formal inference and informal inference.

[12]See Herbert Feigl, "De Principiis Non Disputandum Est," in Max Black (ed.), Philosophical Analysis, (Ithaca, 1950).

[13]Grammar, pp. 216-217.

[14]Grammar, p. 228.

[15]Grammar, p. 228.

[16]Grammar, p. 223.

[17]Grammar, p. 229.

[18]In contrast to Richard Whateley, who considers syllogism to be the whole of logic, Newman states that he conceives generalization to be a form of inference because it implies a conclusion about the similarity of the things generalized. See G.R. Evans, "'An Organon More Delicate, Versatile and Elastic': John Henry Newman and Whateley's Logic," The Downside Review, XCVII (1979), 175-191, for an account of Newman's relation to Whately and the influence of the latter's Elements of Logic on him. Compare those other passages where Newman states that inference is but a kind of intuition. See especially the section on intuition and instinct below. Let me anticipate myself here. A problem that will arise when we come to deal with first principles is this: if first principles are discovered by intuition, and if inference is a form of intuition, then there is a possibility that first principles are not prior to reasoning, despite Newman's repeated claims to the contrary. It is because of this possibility that it is necessary to show that natural inference, which is the only kind of inference which could precede the establishment of first principles, is, in at least one of its aspects, really a form of simple assent.

[19]Grammar, p. 230.

[20]G.P. Klubertanz, S.J., "Where is the Evidence for Thomistic Metaphysics?" Revue Philosophique de Louvain, LVI (1958), p. 295; p. 300.

[21]A.J. Boekraad, The Personal Conquest of Truth according to John Henry Newman (Louvain, 1955.), p. 206.

[22]Jay Newman, "Cardinal Newman's Factory-Girl Argument," Proceedings of the American Catholic Philosophical Association, XLVI (1972), p. 76.

[23]Grammar, pp. 247-248.

[24]Jay Newman, "Factory-Girl," p. 77.

[25]cf. Boekraad, Personal Conquest, pp. 206-210.

[26]Grammar, p. 233.

[27]Cf. the discussions of natural inference and intuition and instinct below.

[28]Grammar, p. 233.

[29]Grammar, p. 233. See also, G. Mavrodes, Belief in God (New York, 1970). Of course ´proof´ in this context cannot be synonymous with ´formal demonstration.´ The structure of a formal inference is perfectly explicit and is intelligible, in principle, to any mind. The structure of an informal inference is neither universally explicit nor universally intelligible. Ferreira comments on pp. 62-63:
This reveals the tension between the concepts of ´personal´ and ´objective´. Newman´s reminder that proof is in some sense person-dependent was not meant to imply that certitude is dependent on what each man thinks is certain since Newman´s avowed intention was to lessen the difficulties which lie in the way of calling (someone) to account for (claims to certainty)´ (196) Thus, Newman seems to have believed that ´personal´ need not be opposed to ´objective´.

In my opinion, certitude is, in a sense, dependent on what each man thinks is certain. Proofs are personal in that the complex of beliefs into which the disputed propositions is to fit is ultimately a product of our first principles. In addition, since there are no paradigms for the universal validation of informal inferences it follows that, even granted the truth of the premises, the inference itself still needs to be appropriated by each individual person and this appropriation is also a personal matter. For a sympathetic account of the personal element in proof from a none-too-sympathetic critic of Newman, see J. Hick, Faith and Knowledge, (Ithaca, 1957), pp. 83-105.

[30]"Truth therefore is not something fundamentally relative, but it takes on, so to say, a secondary aspect of relativity from our moral and intellectual being into which that one, objective truth is taken. This problem, which Newman because of its very difficulty calls a mystery, he attempts to consider. The elements which go to the making up of the problem are the following:

1. Man is endowed with the faculty of reason which is instrumental in the acquisition of truth

2. On the whole men use this faculty well, especially in matters in which their interest in involved

3. Nevertheless, it is an established fact that men do arrive at quite different conclusions regarding the same subjects, even though these are of great importance, as, for example, religion, or even the acquisition of truth itself.

4. Yet truth is something absolute. Of this we are conscious when we possess certainty.

5. Diversity therefore, is not due to any deficiency of reason, or a wrong use of it, but to other factors in ourselves which Newman calls our moral and intellectual being

6. It can be admitted that this problem does not arise in the department of the physical and mathematical sciences, at least not with the same force and clearness. This is all the more apparent ´in the case of short proofs, as the propositions of Euclid.´"

Boekraad, Personal Conquest, pp. 128-129.

[31]Grammar, pp. 234-235.

[32]Grammar, pp. 235-239.

[33]Grammar, p. 239.

[34]Grammar, p. 250.

[35]Newman selects Locke as his dialectical opponent on the question of degrees of assent. His remarks on Locke's 'Ethics of Belief' can be found in the Grammar, pp. 136-139; p. 146. Discussions of the nature and extent of the differences between Newman and Locke on this issue can be found in J.M. Cameron, "Newman and Locke: A Note on Some Themes in an Essay in Aid of a Grammar of Assent," Newman Studien, IX (1974), 197-205; and R.A. Naulty, "Newman's Dispute with Locke," Journal of the History of Philosophy, XI (1973), 453-457; and Jay Newman, "Newman on Strength of Beliefs," The Thomist, XLI (1977), 131-147.

[36]Grammar, p. 251.

[37]Newman's citation of the passage in Butler is as follows: Butler, Analogy of Religion, ed. 1830, pp. 329; 330.

[38]In my opinion, Newman is mistaken here. Every science demands a willingness on the part of its practitioners to be convinced by certain kinds of evidence. I owe this point to a discussion with Desmond Clarke.

[39]Grammar, p. 253.

[40]Grammar, pp. 253-54.

[41]See M.J. Ferreira, Doubt and Religious Commitment (Oxford, 1980), pp. 24-28.

[42]For more on mathematical images, analogies, and comparisons in Newman, see G.R. Evans, "Science and Mathematics in Newman's Thought," The Downside Review, XCVIII, (1978), pp. 247-266.

[43]This paper can be found in H.M. Achaval and J.D. Holmes (eds.), The Theological Papers of J.H. Newman on Faith and Certainty (Oxford, 1976), pp. 17-27.

[44]According to Ferreira, "Newman foreshadowed Harman's conclusion that 'justification is not a matter of derivation from basic principles but is rather a matter of showing that a view fits in well with other things we believe.' Newman would argue that it must not only fit in 'well' but fit in better than anything else." (46) This is all right up to a point. There are coherentist elements in Newman's account. Proximately, what justifies belief x may well be that it 'fits' into our actual noetic structure. But, for Newman, the structure as a whole must be grounded on first principles. Coherence only makes sense as a justificatory procedure if the noetic structure as a whole is ultimately grounded. Newman rejected the notion of a group of of mutually supported propositions, no one of which was foundational. See the fourth chapter for further discussion of this topic.

[45]The reasons we have are such as these
* Men are, under circumstances, to be trusted.
* I never heard anyone doubt that all men die.
* All men affirm it.
* I never saw a man alive who was commonly said to be dead.
* What becomes of men if they do not die and disappear?
* Are funerals solemn mockeries?.
* In whose interest would it be to tell lies in this matter?
* People's grief seems to be sincere.

[46]What makes 'evidentia' relative is not any variation in the apprehension of the internal logical structure of a given 'evidentia' but rather the ability or inability of particular individuals to assent to the elements of that 'evidentia.' In the logical terminology of another age we might say that the relativity is accounted for not by questions of validity but by questions of soundness.

[47]Grammar, p. 209. By calling natural inference 'instinctive' Newman does not mean to imply that it is a common natural ability. Natural inference is instinctive and instinct is "a perception of facts without assignable media of perceiving." Grammar, p. 263.

[48]Grammar, pp. 260-61.

[49]Grammar, p. 261.

[50]Newman notes in passing that the fundamental truths of religion can be defended by an array of logical arguments but that this is commonly not the means by which they are attached to our minds. The grounds on which we hold these truths are commonly felt to be "recondite and impalpable in proportion to their depth and reality." Grammar, p. 204.

[51]Grammar, pp. 268-69.

[52]Grammar, pp. 260-261.

[53]See my account of Plantinga's distinction between grounds and evidence in the fourth chapter.

[54]Achaval and Holmes, p. 90.

[55]It is possible that Newman might have been prepared to insist upon the absolute unconsciousness of the phenomenal grounds and thereby concede the fact that natural inference is not really inference after all. However, it is my opinion that the peasant's ability to feel the force of the phenomenal grounds supplies the minimal required level of consciousness and that this is sufficient to salvage the inferential character of the process.

[56]As we shall see below when I come to deal with the relationship of inference to first principles, this confusion can create difficulties for a correct assessment of the epistemological status of first principles.

[57]Grammar, pp. 265-266.

[58]Grammar, p. 266.

[59]Achaval and Holmes, p. 53.

[60]Achaval and Holmes, p. 53.

[61]Achaval and Holmes, p. 54.

[62]See above, pp. 13-14, where the relevant passage is cited in full.

[63]Boekraad, Personal Conquest, p. 142.

[64]Grammar, p. 67.

[65]Ferreira, pp. 39-43. This is not really a problem. What would be problematic would be the absence of what I have been calling grounds, i.e. the unconsciousness of the varied phenomena which can, in principle, be expressed in propositions.

[66]Ferreira, p. 42.

[67]Ferreira is suspicious of the term ´intuition.´ "Talk about insight´ and ´intuition´ generally seems to misrepresent Newman´s thought precisely in the direction of the ´passive impression made on the mind´ which he strongly rejected." (73)

It should be clear that intuition, as I am using the term here, is not simply a ´passive impression´ but the terminal stage of a spontaneous (instinctive) activity of the mind. Instinct is the active intellect, intuition, the passive. These are distinguishable but not distinct aspects of one and the same process. As I use the term, I intend it not only to cover the ´passive impression´ but also the spontaneous activity of mind preceding and leading up to that impression.

[68]It will also be my contention that the proper way to understand Newman´s first principles is as a species of simple assent. And since simple assents are not arrived at inferentially, it would be inconsistent of Newman to insist on inference as a sine qua non for assent per se. This interpretation is compatible with Newman´s use of the term ´assent.´ In is clear from various contexts that Newman uses the term ´assent´ when what he clearly means is ´complex assent´ or ´reflex assent.´ In a similar fashion he often speaks simply of ´inference´ when it is clear from the context that he means ´formal inference.´ This is the topic of subsequent chapters and it will be developed further in them.

[69]For a full account of Newman on conscience, see A.J. Boekraad and H. Tristram, The Argument From Conscience to the Existence of God (Louvain: 1961); J. Collins, God in Modern Philosophy (Chicago, 1959), pp. 361-366; F.J. Kaiser, The Concept of Conscience According to John Henry Newman (Washington, 1958).

[70]If I refer to it hereafter as an ´argument´ I must not be taken to be contradicting myself. My intention is simply to avoid the tedious proliferation of quotation marks.

[71]Grammar, pp. 95-109.

[72]See Gerald McCarthy´s attempt to reformulate it in precisely these terms. G. McCarthy, "Religion and Certainty," Unpublished Dissertation, (University of Pennsylvania, 1977), pp. 233-246. Sillem has this to say: "The argument is phenomenological and from an investigation of what Newman calls the "phenomenon of conscience" and not metaphysical in character. It is not an argument from the nature of law but from man´s experience of himself as a person." Edward Sillem, The Philosophical Notebooks of John Henry Newman, Vol. II, p. 59., (Hereafter, Notebooks.)

[73]"Newman´s arguments in this book (Grammar) are designed to examine the assent given to the doctrines of natural and revealed religions, and not, primarily, the arguments which issue in beliefs in these doctrines. Thus the question which interests him is not "Is there a God?" but how it is possible for us to give a real assent to the existence of God, and what sort of assent it is." J. Robinson, "Newman´s Use of Butler´s Arguments," The Downside Review, LXXVI (1958) 161-180.

[74]"Proof of Theism" can be found, along with other unpublished papers of Newman, in Notebooks, II, pp. 30-78.

[75]Notebooks, Vol II, p. 33.

[76]Notebooks, Vol. II, p. 35.

[77]Lest it be thought that this is a slip of the pen, I might add that Newman states towards the end of this paper that "The ergo in Descartes´s position, Cogito ergo sum, denotes my power of apprehending the aspects of an idea." He maintained this position also in the Grammar; see pp. 13-14 above. In a striking passage, Newman asserts the isomorphism of what he takes to be three inferences:
> As from <u>sentio</u> I infer the existence of myself, so from <u>conscientiam</u> <u>habeo</u> I infer the existence of God, and again from the phenomena of sense I have the existence of matter. (Notebooks, 78.)

Of course, in none of these three cases is there any real inference at all.

[78]Notebooks, Vol. II, p. 75.

[79]Notebooks, Vol. II, pp. 75-77.

[80]Notebooks, Vol. II, p. 45.

[81]I maintain this despite McCarthy´s claim to the contrary. According to McCarthy, it is clear that the argument from conscience is meant to be an example of an informal inference. He bases his claim on Newman´s prelude to the argument where Newman says that inference is a drawing out of a complex intuition into propositional form. (McCarthy, pp. 199-204). It is difficult to see why McCarthy puts forward this claim, given his clear understanding of what Newman takes himself to be doing in the "argument" from conscience:
> [Newman] argued that the inference from our moral experience to the existence and moral attributes of God is of the same characterp as the inference from "cogito" to "sum"; i.e., it is not primarily an inference at all but rather a "complex intuition." (McCarthy, p. 92)

[82]"Evocation is the process by which vividness is conveyed...It is said that argument is a way by which an individual experience is made common property; in fact, an argument has much less persuasive force than the vivid evocation of an experience...(It is) far more effective to state a viewpoint in all its concreteness and in all its significant implications, and then stop; the arguments become revelant only after this stage has been concluded." (229) R. Demos, "On Persuasion," The Journal of Philosophy, XXXIV (1932) 225-232.

CHAPTER 2

ASSENT, CERTITUDE, AND INTUITION

In this chapter I wish to consider, in so far as
it is possible, what assent is, in and of itself. As
in the first chapter I was concerned with the relationships between the different kinds of inference, so here
I shall concern myself solely with the relationship
between the different kinds of assent. I shall begin
by reviewing what Newman has to say on these matters in
the Grammar, then I shall go on to consider whatever
additional information may be gleaned from his other
writings. Finally, I shall take a brief look at a contemporary writer whose concerns parallel Newman's in an
enlightening way.

Assent

The section on simple assent in the Grammar is
somewhat misleadingly entitled. It has little or nothing to say about simple assent though it tells us quite
a lot about the nature of the relationship between inference and assent.[1] What little Newman does have to
say about simple assent comes at the beginning of the

section on complex assent. There we learn that

> [A]ssent [is] the mental assertion of an intell-
> igible proposition...an act of the intellect
> direct, absolute, complete in itself, uncondit-
> ional, arbitrary, yet not incompatible with an
> appeal to argument, and at least in many cases
> exercised unconsciously.[2]

Assent then has the following characteristics:

1. It is a mental assertion, i.e. an act of the
   mind not necessarily expressed.

2. It is the assertion of <u>an</u> <u>intelligible</u> <u>propos-
   ition</u> which means that it is expressible if
   not actually expressed.

3. It is direct, absolute, complete in itself,
   unconditional. All these words are intended
   to show assent's independence from its circumstances or conditions. Note, however, that
   Newman is careful to say that assent is compatible with argument.

4. Finally, assent is, for the most part, unconscious. The distinction between simple assent
   and complex assent is this: simple assents
   are unconscious; complex assents are
   conscious and deliberate. Most of our assents

are unconscious and hence are simple assents.[3]

My thesis in this chapter is that just as there are two distinct natural inferences: natural inference(1), which is the limiting case of informal inference, and natural inference(2), which is instinctive intuition, so also there are two kinds of simple assent; simple assent(1), which is the concomitant act of assent to natural inference(1), and simple assent(2), which is the concomitant of the instinctive process that is natural inference(2). Strictly speaking, the parallel structure does not obtain since natural inference(2) is intuition. But as we can distinguish within intuition an act and the terminus of that act we can allow natural inference(1) refer to the act and intuition (natural inference (2)) refer to the terminus of that act.[4] Unconsciousness then is a mark which serves to distinguish complex assent as a whole from the class of simple assents as a whole. However, it is not sufficient to distinguish between the different kinds of simple assents. For the moment, let us turn our attention to complex assent or reflex assent.[5]

Certitude

Reflex assent differs from simple assent in that it is explicit and deliberate. It is an assent not only to ´p´ but to the claim of ´p´ on our assent as true. It is an assent to an assent, or a conviction.

> Let the proposition to which the assent is given be as absolutely true as the reflex act pronounces it to be, that is, objectively true as well as subjectively: – then the assent may be called a <u>perception</u>, the conviction a <u>certitude</u>, the proposition or truth a <u>certainty</u>.[6]

This passage reveals three points:

1. The use of the term ´perception´ with reference to the original act of assent will lend support to my claim that simple assent is a kind of intuition.[7]

2. Certitude is a species of assent, namely, reflex or complex assent.

3. Newman would like the term ´certitude´ to be reserved for those, and only those, assents that are in fact true. However, since Newman has to admit the existence of false certitudes, he cannot sustain this claim.[8]

Newman realizes the importance of the problem of distinguishing certitude from persuasion and delusion, so he lists three characteristics which a proposition has to possess to be considered a certitude. First, it has to be a reflex assent, i.e. an assent subsequent to investigation. Second, it has to be accompanied by a _sui generis_ psychological state which Newman calls repose. Third, it must be irreversible. The first of these characteristics of certitude has already been touched upon. The second characteristic, repose, is basically the spontaneous rejection of doubt.[9]

> No man is certain of a truth who can endure the thought of the fact of its contradictory existing or occurring; and that not from any set purpose or effort to reject the thought but...by the spontaneous action of the intellect.[10]

A prime characteristic of certitude is that it cannot co-exist with hesitation or doubt. It follows from this that such a state of mind cannot be immediately dependent on the reasons which are its antecedents and cannot be rightly referred back to them as its producing cause. Newman's point is simple. If certitude were the direct result of testimony, or argument, then objections would weaken it gradually. But certitude does not, in fact, admit of more or less. If twelve witnesses are sufficient to lead me to certainty, then a thirteenth witness is superfluous. Certitude is not to be measured by the logical force of premisses. We cannot say in advance of the event just how many witnesses will be sufficient to create certitude. Whatever the number turns out to be, we are not more certain if we find additional witnesses. The arguments which create certitude in one mind fail to do so in another as if there were no rule external to the individual mind itself of sufficient subtlety to decide the question when it ought to be certain and when not.

Certitude could not exist at all if logical completeness of proof were required as both a sine qua non and a creating cause, that is, as both a necessary and a sufficient condition. It might be argued that certainty should not exist without argumentative cogency but the fact remains that it does and it would be unreasonable to set this standard for its legitimate existence. All this is true of certainty in concrete matter; does it apply to speculative matters too? Here, surely, certainty is the exclusive product of argumentative cogency! Newman denies this. A mathematician does not accept his own demonstration as sufficient for an unconditional assent; it is not the sole preliminary or the immediate instrument of certitude. It is not his demonstration but he himself who makes himself certain. As a matter of fact we find things at the end of demonstrative chains that nothing on earth will persuade us to accept. We are convinced that something must be wrong even though everything looks to be in order. And there are many things about which we are not, in fact certain, since we never think about them at all! We can always deny certitude, even to the conclusion of a cogent chain of reasoning.

Acts of certitude, then, are personal and not the result of scientific antecedents. By this Newman simply means that logically antecedent propositions are not sufficient in and of themselves to create certitude about a given proposition. They are in the power of the individual exercising them and subject to his particular mental constitution. This immediately prompts the question: are these acts of certainty arbitrary acts and in no way directed by reason? Are they simply devoid of any connection with truth and so unmeaning and fruitless? Newman's answer is, No. We hold in our thoughts, without any definite apprehension of it, information conveyed through intuition, pre-possession, teaching, reasoning, testimony, tradition, revelation. When we recognize these thoughts and become certain of them we do not do so arbitrarily but by means of our judgement, our good sense, or our experience, which completes the evidence and determines what it is worth.

> Certitude then is not the passive admission of a conclusion as necessary but the recognition of it as true. It is not the mere acceptance of a conclusion as a conclusion, or of a testimony as a testimony, or of a sensation as a sensation, or of an intuition as an intuition. What is brought home to the mind in whatever way as having an objective existence, this it elevates (whatever it is), into a higher order of thought. It gives it, as it were, an imprimatur, or accords it a registration on the catalogue of things which are to be taken for granted. Or, to keep close to the word itself, the act of certitude is a certifying it or giving a certificate which henceforth will be its passport and its protection. Certitude then, does not come under the reasoning faculty but under the imagination. When I make a act of certitude in the death of Prince Albert, I am contemplating a fact in itself, as presented to me by my imagination, and apart from the means by which I gained it. Sense, logic, authority, testimony, belong to the process; the result is beyond them and independent of them, and stands by itself, as long as I choose, created and dependent on myself as an individual and free agent.[11]

The act of certitude is formally independent of the process by which the proposition is arrived at. Materially, of course, without the process there would be no proposition to certify. An act of certitude is an unconditional assent to a proposition as true. By an assent to a proposition as true Newman means that what the intellect is contemplating subjectively has an existence outside it. The propositions to which the assents of certitude are given are necessarily of a complex form viz., "´a is b´ is true." The act of mind in certitude is reflex, for, as the assertion of a correspondence between what is without and what is within me, it involves a recognition of myself. As such it differs from knowledge which is the simple contemplation of truth as objective. So, we speak of having knowledge and feeling certain. Finally, it is an unconditional assent; we reject the very notion of our being mistaken.

Newman is aware of the objection against the possession of real speculative certainty and he expresses it very forcefully. Speculative certainty must have truth for its object and it must be a conviction of that truth. It is claimed that it cannot be a conviction till it is proved not to be a persuasion, and this proof, Newman says, is beyond us. On the other hand, it cannot claim to have truth for its object, for in concrete matters no proof that we can frame can pass beyond probability, greater or less, according to the measure of the arguments which are adduced for it. Therefore, real certainty, or a state of conviction, or the conscious possession, real mental attainment, and conscious attainment of what is true, is impossible in our present state of being. Newman's response to this problem is typical. He has no irrefutable argument to give in reply. All he can say is that despite the absence of a decisive test between conviction and persuasion (given the merely probable character of the evidence on which our conclusions are based) still we cannot help entertaining a certainty of the truth of things which we are unable to demonstrate. This certainty is not merely practical but really speculative. Backing off one's thesis in the presence of an acknowledged authority, irritation and impatience of contradiction, vehemence of assertion, intellectual anxiety, fussing with arguments, all these are signs of non-certitude. To be sure, they are not infallible signs, for they may arise from the emotions or imagination and need not be intellectual, but in general "to fear argument is to doubt the conclusion and to be certain of a truth is to be careless of objection to it."[12] If our assent is not accompanied by these signs of intellectual irritation it is, by the same token, marked by what Newman calls ´repose.´ This repose or intellectual satisfaction, though similar to other feelings in that it is uniquely associated with a particular mental feature, nevertheless is sui generis. Repose is the mark of certitude as self-approval is the mark of a conscientious deed. The repose Newman has in mind is neither associated with simple assent, nor with inference, nor doubt, nor investigation, nor conjecture, nor opinion. There are peculiar feelings attached to assent, inquiry and doubt, each as indicative of that state as repose is of certitude.

According to Newman, most men pass through life with neither doubt nor certitude, but only with simple assents. Simple assents are now recognized by Newman as being virtual, material, or interpretative (potential) certitudes. Many problems arise with these simple assents. They can be lost while trying to convert them into certitudes. We possess assents which turn

out to be mere prejudices. Some assents are withdrawn.
Other assents deteriorate into professions:

> The event... alone determines what is outwardly
> an assent is really such an act of the mind as
> admits of being developed into certitude, or is
> a mere self-delusion or a cloak for ubnbelief.[13]

I have thus far considered two characteristics of
certitude; reflexivity and repose. Now I turn to its
third and most importance characteristic, persistence,
or as Newman calls it, indefectibility.

Ideally, certitude is a right conviction. Truth
is such that it cannot change. When a mind becomes
possessed of truth, what is to dispossess it? It seems
that once we have a certitude, we should always have
that certitude. The idea of persistence, or indefectibility, almost enters into the idea of certitude such
that if certitude frequently failed, then it would be
shown to be an intellectual extravagance.[14] Newman,
then, takes it as his task to show that, as a rule,
certitudes do not fail. Failures are the exception:
"The intellect...is made for truth, can attain truth,
and having attained it, can keep it, can recognize it
and can preserve the recognition."[15]

There are, however, problems which must be faced. False certitudes may last. Our present convictions may be exchanged for opposite convictions and each can be attended by the characteristic feeling of repose and, of course, be subsequent to a process of investigation. More generally, if we can be wrong in one case why not in another? If it is possible for us to entertain just one false certitude, are we ever justified in entertaining any? Newman acknowledges that these problems arise from the facts of the matter. Men do change their certitudes (or, at least, what they consider to be such.) The question that Newman has to answer is "How is certitude possible if it is so often misplaced; if it is fickle and inconsistent, and if it is deficient in available criteria?"[16]

By way of a response Newman first distinguishes between infallibility and certitude. Part of the problem concerning certitude arises from confusing it with infallibility and expecting of it what can only properly be expected of infallibility. Infallibility is a faculty or gift addressed to all possible propositions in a particular subject-matter, whereas certitude is directed only to particular propositions. Properly speaking, it is persons or rules which are infallible, not propositions though in a broad sense we can speak of a proposition´s being infallible if it is the product of an infallible faculty.

Next, Newman denies that the failure of one particular certitude destroys the possibility of certitude in general. It is true that there is some antecedent difficulty in allowing ourselves to be certain of proposition x if yesterday we gave up proposition y but all this indicates is the necessity for an increase in circumspection concerning the making of certitudes in the first place, not the necessity for making none at all. Certitude is a deliberate assent given after reasoning or investigation. If the certitude is unfounded then it is the reasoning which is at fault, not the certitude. Errors in reasoning are lessons not to give up reasoning altogether but simply to reason with greater caution. Finally, the very possibility of showing a given certitude to be false itself demands the possibility of certitude for we are at least certain now that our previous certitude was misplaced! We were certain that ´p´. We were wrong in this certainty. But we are now certain that "We were wrong to be certain that ´p´". Newman notes that

> [If] functional disarrangements of the intellect
> are to be considered fatal to the recognition of
> the functions themselves, then the mind has   no
> laws whatever and no normal constitution...No
> instances then whatever of mistaken certitude
> are sufficient to constitute a proof, that cer-
> titude itself is a perversion or extravagance.[17]

The problem of the reversal of   certitudes   is   not   as

severe   as it might appear to be, for Newman holds that

most alleged cases of the abandonment of certitude   are

precisely   not   that.   People confuse the probable, the

possible and the certain.   They don´t   distingush   bet-

ween   credence, opinion, profession, etc.   All of these

states are called ´certitude´ and when they   are   aban-

doned   it then seems as if certitude has become defect-

ible.   Furthermore, if we remember that certitude is an

assent   following upon investigation, or proof, then it

becomes clear that the number of genuine certitudes   is

much   smaller than is commonly supposed.   This might be

considered a formal restriction on what can   constitute

a   certitude.   There   are   also material restrictions.

Some areas of knowledge can   properly   provide   propos-

itions   which   can   be   the object of certitude.   Other

areas are less suited to this task.   We can   more   pro-

perly   have   certitudes   about   home,   friends, family,

neighbourhood, than we can concerning   public   affairs,

social or professional life, business, literature, experimental sciences.

What of certitude in the area of religion? It is often put forward as an objection that theology is now in the same state as science was five hundred years ago, i.e. it consists of a set of competing and irreconcilable belief systems. Newman's response is that religion is not simply a proposition or set of propositions but a rite, a creed, a philosophy, a complex of duties. To accept a religion is not simply to assent either simply or complexly to a set of propositions, nor is it to give it notional rather than real assent, nor is it to give it credence rather than profession, or opinion rather than speculation. It is, rather, a complex of various propositional attitudes adopted towards those elements of religion which are propositional. For example, according to Newman, a Protestant holds a variety of propositions, not all of which are certitudes. He has an implicit belief that Scripture is commensurate with Revelation. He professes to believe in the Inspiration of Scripture. He gives a speculative assent to the proposition that those doctrines are true which are proven from Scripture. On the other hand, he gives a real assent to the proposition that the Church has no authority. It is a prejudice of his that the Church is condemned in the Apocalypse. He opines that St. John was the author of the Apocalypse. He accepts, but scarcely apprehends the proposition that justification is by Faith alone. He is certain that our Lord is God.

The conversion of a man from one religion to another is often taken to be prima facie evidence of the defectibility of certitude. According to Newman, we must first ask if the two religions have anything in common. If they have, then the man has exchanged only a portion of what he believed and not all. Next we have to ask ourselves what doctrines he was certain of in the old religion and what he is certain of in the new. Very often, what is abandoned is that which was not in fact held as certain and what was held as certain is retained while other certitudes are added to it. However, there do seem to be cases where prior certitudes have to go. For example, were a Jew to be converted to Catholicism, he would have to yield the certitude that the Mosaic Law is sufficient. Similarly, a Mohommedan would have to give up the certitude that Mohammed is a prophet. Newman could respond here that since certitude is a conviction of what is true and, since these propositions are not true, _ipso facto_, they are not, and never were, certitudes! However, this would be to make an illegitimate use of the strong sense of certitude which Newman has already realized he cannot have. On the other hand, he would be within his rights to insist that these putative certitudes be proven to be more than mere prejudices. Who, Newman asks, is converted? Those who hold these inadmissable certitudes or those who do not? Manifestly, those who do not. What this means of course is that prior to conversion these so-called certitudes are recognized not to be such and never to have been such and so there is no abandonment of certitude in converting.

In the end however, Newman has to allow that certitude admits of no interior immediate test sufficient to distinguish true certitudes from false certitudes.[18] Indefectibility stands as a negative test, a _sine qua non_, such that whoever loses his conviction is thereby proved not to have been certain of it. Unfortunately, since at any given time we do not know which of our stock of certitudes (as we take them to be) is going to fail we cannot use this criterion to distinguish now between those certitudes which are real and those which are apparent.

Newman notes that prejudices may also be indefectible but that they cannot be confused with certitude since the latter is assent after rational grounds while the former is assent prior to rational grounds.[19]

We have seen then that there are three marks or criteria of certitude. Certitude follows upon investigation or proof; it is accompanied by a specific sense of repose or intellectual satisfaction; and it is irreversible.[20] If something purports to be certitude but does not follow upon investigation then it is, in Newman's terms, a prejudice. If it is not accompanied by a sui generis sense of repose then it is inference and not assent. Finally, if it is not irreversible then it is a mere conviction and no certitude.

Intuition

Thus far I have considered assent, and certitude which is one of its specific forms. At the beginning of the chapter I stated that my thesis would be that there exist two forms of simple assent to correspond to

the two forms of natural inference. The existence of a
form of simple assent corresponding to that natural
inference which is the limiting case of informal inference is unproblematic. My task then amounts to showing
the existence of that simple assent which is the terminal state of the other form of natural inference,
namely instinct/intuition. Newman's thought on intuition, its nature and its function, underwent some
development. I shall begin my examination with a consideration of Newman's unpublished paper "Proof of
Theism" which we have already looked at in connection
with the argument from conscience.

Throughout this 1859 paper, Newman has W.G. Ward
in mind whenever he is discussing intuition. Insofar
as he has any reservations about the notion of intuition, it is about that notion as it is to be found in
Ward's works. I have already noted that in the beginning of this paper, Newman puts forward a rough sketch
of a theory of mind. Our faculties are, as it were,
aspects of our being and to speak of either trusting or
doubting them is as much a philosophical solecism as it
is to speak of trusting or doubting our existence.[21]

> I am a unit made up of various faculties,[22]
> which seem to me parts of my being and to be as
> much facts as that being itself -- and, as it

would be improper to say that I <u>believe</u> in my being...so it seems to me an improper use of terms and a play upon words to say that I have faith in these faculties, their exercise and their dictates....if it be improper to speak of <u>faith</u> in one's being it is improper to speak of <u>faith</u> in (certain) other things besides being -- because being is not know directly, but indirectly through its states.[23]

Let us digress for a moment to consider McCarthy's discussion of this topic in Newman. According to McCarthy, Newman argued that we must assume that natural processes will lead us to the truth.[24] In McCarthy's estimation, this argument is implausible since it fails to account for the presence of prejudice. Newman, it seems, gives two arguments. The first argument is that our faculties are part of ourselves and therefore it makes as much sense to speak of trusting our faculties as it does to speak of trusting ourselves. The second argument is that we use our faculties, and, therefore, it is improper to speak of trusting them. Against the first argument McCarthy suggests that it is mere metaphor to say that our faculties are part of ourselves and this metaphor is unable to bear the weight necessary to assimilate self-referring statements to statements concerning the evidential status of sensory reports. Against the second argument McCarthy suggests that we have no reason to think that using something is incompatible with trusting it. We use many instruments and we trust them!

Concerning the first of Newman's arguments, it is simply not the case (pace McCarthy) that Newman is assimilating self-referring statements and statements about the evidential status of sensory reports, if by the latter is meant particular statements about the epistemic worth of particular sensory reports. Concerning the second Newman argument, McCarthy's counter-example will not do. We have a choice over whether or not we will use particular conventional tools; we have no choice over whether or not we use sense, memory and reason. This is Newman's point. Since 'trust' is a concept properly used in contexts where a legitimate choice exists it makes no sense to speak of trusting our faculties. Note also, that in these passages, Newman is speaking of sense, memory and reason as faculties: he is not asserting the evidential inviolability of particular deliverances (acts) of these faculties. This distinction between act and faculty deflates most of McCarthy's criticism.

McCarthy goes on to note the type difference between (1) statements about the evidential status of our
particular sensory experience, and (2) statements about
the evidential status of all our sensory experience.
He accuses Newman of failing to grasp this distinction
and of presenting the following argument:

1. to doubt all our sensory experience leads to
   scepticism

2. therefore, we can trust any particular one of
   our sensory experiences.

In response to this accusation I can only repeat
that Newman does not make the type mistake. As I indicated above, he is keenly aware of the difference
between statements referring to the status of particular sensory experience and statements referring to the
status of sensory experiences as a class. Also, I cannot find in any of Newman's writings the arguments that
McCarthy attributes to him, either in substance or in
spirit. The passages that McCarthy adverts to in Newman do not support the argument that McCarthy gives.
In fact, the opposite is the case.

We are as little able to accept or reject our
mental constitution, as our being. We have not

> the option; we can but misuse or mar its
> functions....therefore, I cannot call the trust-
> worthiness of the <u>faculties</u> of memory and rea-
> soning one of our <u>first principles</u>.[25]

Here, Newman is clearly talking about faculties. The
fact that we must use our faculties in no way implies
that our use is always correct. This quotation clearly
shows that Newman recognizes the distinction between
our faculties and the particular acts of our faculties.
Newman claims that it is senseless to speak of trusting
our powers of reason, memory and sense, but he does not
(at least not here) claim that it is senseless to trust
or distrust the particular deliverances of reason,
sense and memory. In another passage adverted to by
McCarthy, Newman says:

> As memory is not always accurate...as our senses
> at times deceive us...so it is also with our
> reasoning faculty.[26]

Is McCarthy under the impression that this text supports his claim?

Of the pages adverted to by McCarthy in <u>Notebooks</u>
I find nothing at all on page 24 concerning our topic!
Page 204 deals with instinctive convictions and first
principles, and its citation by McCarthy is further
proof that he is not aware of Newman's position on intuition as I have outlined it.

In summary, these passages do not support McCarthy's claim that Newman failed to distinguish between act and faculty. It is, in fact, clear from the citations that Newman was well aware of this difference. Neither do the citations support the claim that Newman presented the arguments that McCarthy claims he did. These arguments are nowhere to be found in Newman's texts, either explicitly or implicitly. Newman did <u>not</u> fail to distinguish act from faculty. Newman did <u>not</u> argue that the senselessness of either trusting or distrusting our faculties automatically implied the trustworthiness of any particular act of our faculties.

Let us now return to our discussion of Ward.[27] He defends what he calls "intuitive judgements" against the sceptic. These intuitive judgements are propositions based on reasoning and memory and Wards claims, against the sceptic, that

> Unless I can trust my various acts of memory, I don't even know what the sceptic <u>says</u>, much less what he <u>means</u>. But if I <u>can</u> trust these acts of memory then certain intuitive judgements may with reason be confidently be formed.[28]

Newman thought it absurd to speak of trusting our faculties and so was chary of Ward's "intuitive judgements." His reluctance to use of the word 'intuition' arose because he felt that in using it he might be taken to be endorsing Ward's particular theory of mind.

Now, in "Proof of Theism," Newman also refers to 'perception' and it is clear from the context that this 'perception' is what I have been calling 'intuition.' I have indicated why he felt it necessary to avoid the term 'intuition' and it is not unreasonable to suppose that 'perception' is its substitute.

> What is called reasoning, then is in its essence not a deduction, but it is the perception of certain complex ideas, or the modes or the dress of things.[29]

Towards the end of this paper, when he attempts to explain more precisely what this 'perception' is, he has explicit recourse to the term 'intuition'.

> That one man sees what another does, that A & B are alike arise from no comparison & discrimination of outlines, complexion, features, etc. but it arises from the way in which he...looks at them. It is a kind of intuition, hence it is very difficult to separate what is called reasoning from intuition.[30]

Newman lists 'reasoning' as one of those primary constituents of consciousness in and through which my existence is made known to me. Other such constituent acts are memory, sensation, conscience. etc. However, even though all these are revelatory of my existence, nevertheless reasoning is _primus_ _inter_ _pares_.

> Whereas the consciousness I possess that I exist may be drawn out into "I am _for_ I feel" "I am _for_ I remember", "I am _for_ I think", "I am _for_ I reason," in all cases there is the ´_for_´ or the consciousness of the presence of that condition in which the coincidence of the initial and secondary object of consciousness depends. I am conscious I exist ´in that´ I feel; but this ´in that´ is what is commonly called a reason, or the symbol of an act of reasoning.[31]

Here Newman makes a mistake whose existence he so clearly recognized in the Grammar, namely that of expressing a fact in the form of an argument and mistaking it for an argument thereafter.[32] The ´_for´s´_ in the examples above are not expressive of any real act of inference; rather, they express the original condition(s) in and through which I am aware of my existence. If these examples were re-phrased in the Cartesian manner Newman would have had no difficulty in recognizing the absence of inference. Of the propositions "I feel, therefore I am," "I remember, therefore I am," etc., Newman would have to say what he says of Descartes´s Cogito, namely, that it is no argument but merely the expression of a ratiocinative instinct.[33]

What misleads Newman here and throughout all his work is the partial isomorphism between intuition and inference. As in inference we have a bipartite structure (premisses, and the conclusion based on those premisses) so too in intuition we have grounds (or, as Newman calls them here, conditions) and that which is based upon those grounds. Here the isomorphism ends. For while inference is a relationship between propositions, intuition is a ´relationship´ between our experience and judgements which are expressive of properties of that experience. I deliberately put ´relationship´ in quotes for while in inference the premisses and conclusion are really distinct items of the same kind and thus, really relatable, in intuition, the grounds or conditions of the judgement and the judgement itself are not distinct in quite the same way. Premisses and conclusion are the same in that they are all propositions; they are different in that they are different propositions. Grounds, and the judgements based on those grounds, are the ´same´ in that one is a onto-psychological entity and the other is the propositional expression of that entity. They are different in that they are different kinds of entity.

Newman is reluctant to accept the term 'intuition.' He would like to confine the use of the term
'intuition' to internal acts only.

> What is internal to the mind is an object of
> consciousness, which external things are not.
> Thus the line is broad & deep between the re-
> liance on reason or conscience and upon the
> trustworthiness of the impressions of the senses
> or the reality...of matter. Hence the being of
> a God arising out of what is internal, is an
> external fact different in evidence (proof) from
> every other external fact.[34]

However, Newman is not being consistent here.
Conscience is, in his terms, an object of consciousness. So too, however, is sensation. Neither of
these, _qua_ faculties or modes of mind, are taken on
trust or faith, they are simply coeval aspects of our
being in and through which we experience that being.
Both conscience and sensation have intentional aspects.
The intentional aspect of the former leads us to recognize the existence of God: the intentional aspect of
the latter leads us to recognise the existence of the
external world. Newman cannot have it both ways. If
he denies the intentional aspect of sensation, he must
deny it of conscience. Newman seems to be aware of the
difficulty and tries to avoid it:

> I have a sensation of colours and forms -- this
> is one thing. I have a persuasion that these
> colours and forms convey to me the presence of

> external objects -- this is a second thing, I
> have said that the sensation is not an object of
> faith, but of consciousness -- but the second is
> an object of faith. Its (truth) is not bound up
> in that act of consciousness by which I know I
> am.[35]

Unfortunately, this, if said of conscience, would, by

parity of reasoning, destroy Newman´s premier argument.

Newman has no grounds upon which to distinguish between

conscience and sensation and so is not entitled to

restrict intuition to internal acts only.

A year later, considering these matters in a

non-polemical context, Newman modified his thought.[36]

Assent, he says, is either absolute and simple, or con-

ditional and complex. Absolute or simple assent is the

recognition of the truth of a thought on its own acc-

ount, and independently of everything else...it is an

assent to what I see to be self-evident. Such is the

assent given to "Truth is praiseworthy",

"Self-preservation is a duty." Conditional or complex

assent is that which I give to a thought as true viewed

with and within another thought. "God must be omni-

scient´ in that He is God. "The Creator has power over

his works" because it is his work. Simple and absolute

assent may also be called intuition, being an insight

into things as they are.

> I have considered it (an intuition) to be my
> assent to a truth on its own account, independ-
> ently of any thing external to it; or the
> direct insight which I personally possess (so
> far forth) into things as they are. In other
> words, it is the vision, analogous to eye-sight,
> which my intellectual nature has of things as
> they are, arising from the original elementary
> sympathy or harmony between myself and what is
> external to myself, I and it being portions of
> one whole, and, in a certain sense, existing for
> each other.[37]

Complex assent Newman terms ´contuition´ as being a

sight of a thing through and by means of the things

which lie about it. Examples: Any belief in the moral

law is an intuition, and any belief in its penalties is

a contuition. Intuition is frequently taken to mean an

assent to a truth which does not admit of proof, but

this is not so always. For example, Catholics are

bound to admit that the being of God can be proved by

reason yet some among them hold that it is an intuitive

truth.

Now, the question immediately arises as to whether

this distinction between absolute assent (simple

assent/intuition) on the one hand and conditional as-

sent (complex assent/contuition) on the other is equi-

valent to the simple assent/complex assent distinction

of the Grammar? On first glance they seem to overlap

nicely but then one´s attention is caught by the word

´conditional´ as applying to assent. In the Grammar, assent is strictly defined as being unconditional. What then is this ´conditional´ assent? From the examples given ("God must be omnipotent in that He is God"; "The Creator has power over his works because He is the Creator") it is clear that this ´conditional´ assent is a form of inference. So, the distinction in "Assent and Intuition" does not coincide with that of the Grammar. This reading of the distinction between intuition and contuition further confirms my thesis regarding the relationship between intuition and inference, their structural isomorphism and their material difference. This will become clearer as we work through the passage. Throughout the passage, I shall insert the word ´inference´ in parentheses after every occurence of the term ´contuition´ so as to render the meaning more perspicuous.

Although he holds that intuition and contuition (inference) are clearly distinct Newman nevertheless notes the practical difficulties of telling, in particular circumstances, whether we are dealing with intuition or contuition (inference). Assent is given to what is self-evident, specially to me, though I have not before my mind any actual proof of it. As such it is relative both to me and to my circumstances. We may call the subject and his circumstances the conditions of that assent, noting as we do so that neither the subject nor his circumstances are propositions. On the other hand, in contuition (inference), that truth (true proposition) which comprises the special object of my assent, may be so wide and familiar, or so evidently obvious, as merely to constitute the medium, or condition of my assent. Unlike the former case, truth, at least in epistemological circumstances, is necessarily embodied in propositions. Thus, Newman continues, both intuition and contuituion may stand for an assent upon a condition but in the one case the condition or conditions are not propositions and in the other case they are.

The example Newman gives is interesting. "There is an unseen world: this I cannot deny <u>for</u> <u>the</u> <u>phen-</u> <u>omena</u> <u>of</u> <u>sense,</u> <u>of</u> <u>which</u> <u>I</u> <u>am</u> <u>conscious,</u> <u>imply</u> <u>some-</u> <u>thing</u> <u>beyond</u> <u>the</u> <u>object</u> <u>of</u> <u>sense</u>." The italicized words are a condition. This truth is an intuition, to me, as a being of five senses, who assents according to the conditions or circumstances of his state: i.e. it

is an intuition if it is not made on the basis of propositions. But it is a contuition (inference) if I
directly contemplate the phenomena of sense, and that
which they imply (viz. propositions) when I make the
assertion that an unseen world exists, and include it
in my assent.[38]

McCarthy claims that Newman finds it difficult to
sustain the distinction between intuition and contuition (inference) and he finds this fact to be significant. In discussing the question of whether our perceptual beliefs are the results of inference he writes:

> [R]egardless of whether we are willing to
> classify simple acts of perception as inference,
> the fact remains that they can be thrown into
> inferential form upon reflection.[39]

From this it follows (McCarthy thinks) that in regard
to a proposition expressing a perceptual belief we cannot tell whether that proposition expresses a simple
perceptual belief or a complex perceptual belief. This
fact prevented Newman from adopting the full intuit-
ionist position.

McCarthy's mistake is instructive. He has failed
to notice that our perceptual beliefs are analytically
equivalent to the propositions which can be expressive

of our experience. If I claim "there is a red object in front of me" the basis of the claim is my experience of there being a red object in front of me and not the proposition "I am being appeared to red-objectly." The independence which simple assents or intuitions possess is independence of such propositions. With regard to complex assent or contuition (inference), Newman's examples clearly shows the presence of those other propositions with and within which the proposition assented to are to be found. Simple assent or intuition is grounded on experience - proponible experience to be sure but nevertheless, experience - and not propositions. Complex assent is located with and within other propositions. It is a kind of intuition (hence Newman's name for it) with this difference that its immediate ground is not experience but other propositions.

Having, as he thinks, clearly established the difference between intuition and contuition (inference), Newman goes on to propose a tentative criterion for an intuition. An intuition is that to which the testimony is uniform and universal. What is assented to by all men in all ages is a right assent and the thing assented to as self-evident is true. Again, the old problem arises. This is a purely descriptive criterion. As such it probably fits nothing. Are we to allow the obduracy of the obtuse to rule out of court that which we hold to be self-evident? If not, then of course we shall have to inject some normative force into our criterion, e.g., an intuition is that which is held by all men in all ages, and we can discount person x and age y because.......because what? Because they were not in a position to know? Because they were morally corrupt?.

Newman is aware of the dubious character of this proposed criterion. He admits its plausibility but wants to examine it more closely. To begin with, there is a problem in regard to its own epistemological status. Is it itself an intuition? If it is not, then it takes for granted various previous propositions without proof. E.g., it assumes that <u>what</u> <u>nature</u> <u>attests</u> <u>or</u> <u>enunciates</u> <u>is</u> <u>true</u>. This principle is not universally accepted. It assumes as self evident that <u>all</u> <u>human</u> <u>minds</u> <u>have</u> <u>one</u> <u>nature</u>. This principle is far from being self evident. Our criterion also assumes that <u>in</u> <u>this</u> <u>one</u> <u>nature</u> <u>are</u> <u>many</u> <u>minds</u>. Again, this

principle is not beyond dispute and has, in fact, been
disputed. Another assumption of the criterion is that
there is a nature external to the mind. The denial of
this assumption is not patently absurd, especially.
not to Christians who hold that there was a time when
the world did not exist. The fifth assumption on which
our criterion rests is the mind is able to reach objective realities.

Now we come to an interesting brief section on
first principles and intuitions where Newman advances
the standard regress argument which is intended to demonstrate the necessity of first principles.

> If we are to advance to conclusions of any kind
> and extend the range of our knowledge, we are
> obliged to recognize certain assents as the
> primary premisses of our investigations and
> their results, and as self evident neither re-
> quiring nor admitting of proof. They are more-
> over present to our natural discernment, con-
> genial to our minds, and claiming our homage
> though they were simply barren and nothing came
> of them. This is the obvious argument for the
> existence of intuition.[40]

That there are such primary premisses almost everyone
agrees; what those primary premisses are very few can
agree upon. Newman re-iterates his conviction that
these primary premisses exist. He claims to have maintained their existence steadfastly.

Newman touches on this topic only briefly since it is not of immediate concern to him and then proceeds to discuss several tests which are offered for the discernment of intuitions. (1) Intuitions are to receive universal assent; (2) they are to be irresistible; and (3) they are to be immediate. Newman notes, very accutely, that the first and second tests imply each other; if an intuition is irresistible then all men will hold it, and if all men hold it, then it must be because of the force with which it addresses the human mind. There are some truths which are universal/irresistible. e.g. consciousness of self, belief in things external to self, assent to the truth that a thing cannot both be and not be. But although there are other intuitions which their supporters claim should be universal and irresistible, there are very few which in fact are so. Newman concludes that if, to be an intuition, an assent must be universal and irresistible, the first principles on which our general knowledge rests are scanty indeed.

Newman has been speaking of intuitions in relation to the tests of universality and irresistibility. In some papers from the years 1861-1863 he considers the

requirement of immediacy.[41] Consider our belief in our
identity and our belief in the stability of the laws of
nature. The second of these beliefs is scarcely universal, and even were it universal, it is not immediate. So much we would all grant. But Newman goes on
to deny that our belief in our identity is immediate,
for at least it is through our mental acts, if not
because of the reflection of our mind upon the fact of
their existence that we hold that belief. In any case,
previous reflection and some previous mental acts, are
necessary conditions of the intuition. "We see our
identity or personality in our seeing, or remembering,
etc."

Newman alludes to the patent fact of cultural re-
lativism, and concludes, that universality of reception
is in no sense necessary to the absolute assent which
we give to certain truths.

Intuition, though it is the absolute assent which
we are naturally capable of giving to the first principles of all knowledge, may be exercised on other
truths; it is the gift of the few as well as of the
multitude. There is no limit to the number of possible
intuitions. Indeed, things which are ordinarily known

by reasoning, may, by some men, be ascertained by intuition.[42] Newman's favorite example of this is Newton's perusal of Euclid on his first going up to Cambridge. It is alleged he was astonished that anyone would bother to write a book about such obvious matters!

> That one community or race, that separate individuals should hold as intuitive, what many others, or the mass of men, do not so hold, is no difficulty, for it may imply nothing else than a deficit in intellectual capacity on the part of those who are blind to it. If intuition be a mental gift or faculty, admitting of degrees, as the faculty of correct deduction admits of degrees, then universality of reception not only need not be, but never can be, a property of intuitive truth, unless it is also accounted as property of deductive. Mere insensibility to an intuition is not a denial of it. The case is the same as regards irresistibility. Not only then is it not startling but it is even reasonable and congrous to maintain, that intuitions are neither irresistible nor universal.[43]

But what happens when one professed intuition is contradictory to another. What are we do to do when those who have least claim to be considered advanced disown our intuitions and maintain others to which we are altogether blind? What of the case where two professed intuitions seem to fall under one common principle yet one part of mankind is capable only of apprehending the first intuition while another part of mankind is capable only of apprehending the second? An example of the first difficulty would be the motion of the sun. To a child or uneducated person the motion of the sun across the sky seems as intuitive a truth as the existence of matter. The evidence of the senses appears to contradict the pronouncements of science. An example of the second difficulty (in which our intuitions are disowned and others are maintained in their place) is the practice of the natives described by Captain Cook, especially their habit of eating in absolute isolation from each other. Cook writes:

How a meal, which every where else brings families and friends together, came to separate them here, we often inquired, but could never learn. They eat alone, they said <u>because</u> <u>it</u> <u>was</u> <u>right</u>; but <u>why</u> it was right to eat <u>alone</u>, they never attempted to tell us: such, however, was the force of <u>habit</u>, that they <u>expressed</u> <u>the</u> <u>strongest</u> <u>dislike</u>, and even <u>disgust</u>, at our eating in society, especially with our women, and of the same victuals. At first we thought this strange singularity arose from <u>some</u> <u>superstitious</u> <u>opinion</u>; but they constantly <u>affirmed</u> <u>the</u> <u>contrary</u> ...Even two brothers and two sisters have each their separate baskets, with provision and the apparatus of their meal ... When we sat down to table, they would go out, sit sit down upon the ground, at two or three yards distance from each other, and, turning their faces different ways, take their repast without interchanging a word.[44]

As an example of the third difficulty, consider this. We are inclined to scoff at those who profess abhorrence at the thought of eating beef or pork, yet how does this abhorrence differ from our own at the thought of eating human-flesh? On what grounds are we to distinguish the one case from the other? It seems that, on principle, one should either eat no meat or eat every variety of meat. In refusing to eat human flesh, are we being merely whimsical or capricious?

> What are we to say to those contrarieties in first principles between man and man? Truth is one and the same; a thing cannot be and not be; if nature tells me that cannibalism is unnatural how is it that races of men practice it without any sense of its being wrong. If I see and touch matter, and it is self evident to me that I do so, does it not turn my head, to use that familiar phrase, to be told by clearsighted and subtle philosophers, that after all, it is not at all clear that matter has any existence?[45]

Newman admits that intuition, though an insight into things as they are, does not necessarily see all that there is to see. Intuitions may be partial and complementary. Indeed, given our limitations as human beings, it is likely that they will be so.

> There seems to me nothing inconsistent or absurd, in holding that rude nature has one insight into things as they are, and that cultivated nature has another; that these separate conditions (states) of the mind partly oppose, and partly support each other; that each has its own advantages and its own wants; that there are truths which the one sees and the other does not; that there are others, which are seen by both of them; that there may be illusions in untaught nature as well as educated; and obstinate prejudice in the exper-

ienced as well (as) wisdom.[46]

In another paper written in 1859[47] Newman had puzzled over this problem of the apparent relativity of intuitions. Different people can, and do, look at the same thing in different ways. These different viewings can, of course, be complementary, i.e. I can see certain selected aspects of x and you can see other selected aspects of x. It is obvious that this account of 'perception' implies a correlative account of the nature of things such that they allow of being thus selectively perceived.[48] Newman does, in fact, have such an account. In the Idea of a University he writes:

> All that exists...forms one large system or complex fact and this resolves itself into an indefinite number of particular facts which...have countless relations of every kind, one towards another.[49]

The objective world is one great fact and the sciences are but partial views of it. These separate abstractions of the original whole constitute the matter of the sciences. The capacity to abstract or to view aspects of objects are one and the same thing. All men possess this capacity to some extent. Its exercise by some men, e.g. Newton, amounts to genius.

How is this capacity exercised? Experience is indeed the occasion of the exercise of this faculty, but it is not its principle. Its principle resides in the judgement we form of the incommunicability or want of relation between certain attributes (even though they are consistent and unite in that unity to which they belong.) So, though we begin with the idea of only one whole or system, we are obliged to view the individual before us as made up of many systems. Why are we under this obligation? Because "with all its capabilities, the human mind cannot take in this whole vast fact at a single glance, or gain possession of it at once.[50] So, our inability to view the "summa rerum"[51] as a whole is a consequence of the limitations of our finite human nature. Were we gods we could grasp the whole in a single glance. But our condition is far from being divine; we are, as Newman puts it, more like "short-sighted readers" than we are like gods.

Given that the original unity presents a manifold of aspects, some of which are consistent with, and in definite relations, to each other, there are certain ways of seeing things that are common to all men.

However, the original unity also possesses aspects which are not immediately evident, i.e. do not lie on the surface. These real aspects will not be perceived by just anyone. It takes originality or genius to perceive them. It is also the case that there is a ´perception´ of aspects that have no objective existence in the original unity. This Newman calls ´ingenuity´ and it is to be contrasted with ´originality.´

Finally, in a letter written in 1861[52] Newman recognizes the fact that our belief in the existence of the external world is an intuition. The reservations he expressed in "Proof of Theism" have disappeared.

> I certainly grant the instinct in our minds by which we spontaneously believe and cherish, as a first idea, that matter exists, (our impression of things derived thro´ the sense are not merely subjective)....I consider that the fact of that instinct is (sufficient to convince us) that (it does exist)....But any how it can hardly be called properly a proof. Considered as an instinctive convinction [sic] or what is often called an intuition, it is not a conclusion but a first principle or premiss, and the existence of matter is not proved, but assumed.[53]

This makes my case in regard to two points. First, Newman clearly acknowledges that belief in the existence of the external world is an intuition. Second, he recognizes that intuitions are not conclusions based on premisses but rather first principles or primary premisses. Looking back, we can recognize a definite progression in Newman's thought on intuition from the earlier writings in which he was reluctant to extend its use to external matters to the present text where he clearly recognises its distinction from inference and its objective reference.

We have seen how in "Proof of Theism" Newman wished to restrict intuition to internal matters only. This desire is simply a manifestation of a deeper and more pervasive tension in Newman's work which can be expressed by the question "How much in thought is contributed by the sense and how much by the mind alone?" Does all thought come ultimately from the senses or does the thinking principle have any power of origination?[54] According to Newman, the thinking principle does have an originative power. The senses do not suggest anything when taken by themselves. The objects presented by the senses are unmeaning until they are interpreted by the mind. The mind interprets out of its own resources. The ideas of order, arrangement, whole and part, for example, seem to be original to the mind.

In another paper from the year 1859[55] Newman elaborates on this. His object is to discover what, if anything, are the elementary and primary principles or conditions of thought. He notes immediately that thinking needs external stimuli. Were the mind to be held incommunicado "it would pass this life in a state of torpor."[56] But external stimuli are necessary to some thoughts merely as occasions for their being elicited. Once aroused, the mind can gain ideas quite independently of the external world. As examples of such ideas, Newman instances the following: unity, individuality and independent existence (gained from a contemplation of itself); totality and part (gained from the contemplation of its various faculties or modes); rule and subjection (gained from the evident subjection of some faculties to others); power and causation (gained from volition and its effects); and time (gained from the lack of coincidence of ideas). These ideas all arise in the mind alone and are independent of any substantial contribution from the senses.[57] Newman does not want to over-emphasize the part the mind plays so he adverts to the fact that a great deal is gained from sense without any origination of the part of the mind. In addition, he refers to a certain circularity. Although the mind interprets sense experience by the power of its own ideas, still, we use the information of sense experience to interpret the experience of mind. For example, the feeling of conscience is one of a specific kind that cannot be described except by analogy from sensible experience. Newman wants to keep open the question of whether all our determinations, principles of arrangement, forms of thought, etc., come from sensible experience or the mind alone. There is a tension in Newman's thought which is ultimately not resolved.[58]

In the final part of this chapter I am going to consider the work of a contemporary author whose problems (and, more importantly, whose solutions to those problems) are strikingly similar to Newman's.

Plantinga on Basic Propositions

Alvin Plantinga presents a doctrine of 'basic beliefs' which, in some of its aspects, is equivalent to what, in Newman, I have been calling intuition.[59] A basic belief is defined as a proposition which I believe but which I do not believe on the basis of any other proposition. Planginga is particularly concerned to show that belief in God meets the requisite criteria for being a basic belief. The crucial notion in his whole enterprise is, of course, that of a basic belief. Let us see what Plantinga means by this.

To begin with, Plantinga ´enthusiastically concurs´ that belief in God is properly basic. His clarification and defense of this contention takes the form of the following four theses:

1. If a person holds belief in God to be properly basic, that person is not thereby committed to the absurd view that just any belief is properly basic.

2. Although belief in God is properly basic it is not groundless.

3. A person who accepts belief in God as properly basic is open to arguments against this belief.

4. This view of basic beliefs does not lead to a kind of fideism.

Of these four points, only the second and third will concern us here. The fourth point will be indirectly discussed in chapter four below.

To begin with, it is important to note that a belief's being properly basic does not mean that it is thereby groundless, i.e. proper basicality does not imply groundlessness. Let us take some examples of basic beliefs: "I see a tree," "I had breakfast today," "My friend is in pain." These beliefs are typically taken to be basic but they are manifestly not groundless. I have an experience on the basis of which I believe that I see a tree. This belief is not held on the basis of other beliefs and so is basic. But it does have a ground, viz., the seeing-of-the-tree. Plantinga distinguishes (a) support from propositions, which he calls evidence, from (b) support from experience, which he calls grounds. Having evidence for a proposition eliminates its basicality; having grounds does not.[60]

It should be readily apparent that this distinction between grounds and evidence is akin to the distinction I have been drawing between intuition and inference. Just as for Plantinga the support for basic beliefs is not provided by other propositions, so too, for Newman, inference is supported by propositions while intuition is grounded in the pre-verbal element in our experience.

For each basic belief we have some justifying circumstances. "In condition C, S is justified in taking P as basic." Of course, these conditions vary with P, and, indeed, the whole business rests on a mass of standard or tacit conditions (ceteris paribus) including, at times, beliefs!

According to Plantinga, while belief in God is properly basic, it too has justifying grounds. Many experiences can call forth belief in God, e.g. the experience of guilt, gratitude, danger, perception of the pattern of the universe. What the experience grounds in each case is not, of course, "God exists" simpliciter, but "God disapproves of what I have done," "God forgives me," etc., where God is the subject of a particular sentence. Strictly speaking, it is these propositions which are properly basic, and not the proposition "God exists." However, since "God exists" is analytically derivable from these propositions which are properly basic, it can be called basic in an extended sense of that term.[61] Plantinga makes an analogy between belief in God and belief in the existence of external objects. We have the following pattern: the 'tree-appearing' experience grounds the properly basic proposition "I see a tree" from which the proposition "There are trees" is analytically derivable. It is interesting to note that Newman also detects a similar grounding pattern in both sensory experience and conscience. We have certain experiences of conscience in which we detect the presence of God as a correlative to the perceived character of the experience. Similarly, when we reflect on our sensory experience, we are led to recognize the existence of the external world which is its source. It is important to note that Newman is not claiming that either conscience or sensation is comprehensively translucent. Conscience reveals the existence of God only under a specific aspect. The remainder of Plantinga's paper is not immediately relevant to the present topic but I include it here since it bears on matters which will concern us in chapter four, namely, the epistemological status of intuitions/basic beliefs.

A question now arises as to the status of these basic beliefs in our noetic structure. Are they, for example, indefeasible? Well, to begin with, internal criticism is always relevant to our noetic structure, including its basic beliefs. For example, if A holds that Gods exists and it also follows from other beliefs that he holds, via rules of inference that he adheres to, that God does not exist, then his noetic structure is defective and something must be done to remedy it. But though it is obvious that <u>some</u> alteration must be made it is not so obvious <u>where</u> it should be made. We could, for example, delete one or other of the conflicting beliefs or even, more drastically, the inferential procedures that make the contradiction possible!

Suppose I have a basic belief. May I hold onto it no matter what occurs? Not according to Plantinga. The justifying conditions which ground our basic beliefs are only <u>prima</u> <u>facie</u>, i.e. they are defeasible. Experience X grounds the proposition ´x´: the burden of proof is shifted to those who wish to deny ´x´. But suppose I discover that I suffer from the dreaded Dendrological disorder (whose victims see trees everywhere) or, in the case under discussion, that you give me an argument with ´-x´ as its conclusion which has premisses that are acceptable to me and which proceeds via logical steps which also are acceptable to me. This would be a defeater for my basic belief. But defeaters are themselves only _prima facie_ defeaters. They too can be defeated, e.g. by spotting defects in the premisses or the inference, or by learning that someone else has done so, on good authority.

Now, it is important to note that if ´x´ is a basic belief for me, and I defeat one of its defeaters, that defeat is _not_ evidence for my belief.

> If I accept a belief A as basic and then encounter a defeater ¯for A, rationality may require that if I continue tō believe A, then I rationally believe there is a defeater for the defeater; but it does not require that I believe A on the basis of that belief. It may be that the conditions under which a belief A is properly basic for me, include my rationally holding some other belief B, but it doesn´t follow that if I am in these conditions then A is not properly basic for me.[62]

This is very close to Newman on assent/inference, viz., that A can be the conclusion of an argument does not mean that I accept A inferentially. To assent to A is (in Plantinga´s terms) to take it as a basic belief. To believe A on the basis of B is, for Newman, to infer it. To believe A _simpliciter_ is to assent to A, even though we may as a matter of fact have arrived at A via B and even though there is a potential inferential chain connecting them.

The conditions that confer prima facie justification do not inevitably include belief. What justifies me in believing that there is a tree in front of me is just the experience, and not the belief that I am thus being appeared to.63

Some experiences confer prima facie justification only because of their associated standing conditions. Suppose I were to come across this headline in the paper: "Dallas slaughters Cincinnati." Part of my justification for this belief is the knowledge that there are such National Football League teams as Dallas and Cincinnati. Without these standing beliefs (contextual beliefs) all I would be justified in believing would be that entity ´Dallas´ whatever it is has slaughtered entity ´Cincinnati´ whatever that is. It might be objected that all our language, including the verbs, are part of the standing contextual conditions. And since it is the experience in conjunction with the contextual conditions that justifies the basic belief, so, in some sense, basic beliefs are derived from other

beliefs, since the contextual conditions are, or seem
to be, at least a necessary condition of our coming to
hold the basic belief. How does the non-verbal ground
the verbal? Surely it can only be through the medium
of language. This would indicate that contextual
beliefs play a more significant role in the grounding
process than Plantinga is willing to allow. It is difficult to sustain any strong notion of basicality in
view of the possibility that the same basic experience
in the presence of different contextual beliefs could
ground a different basic belief. This seems to indicate that experience, of itself, is essentially neutral.
It takes its character from the context in which it is
located. Plantinga wants to maintain that even though
I arrive at a belief on the basis of a certain experience in the context of certain other beliefs, still
these contextual beliefs do not provide part of the
basis for holding that belief. One can see why he has
to maintain this, for the contextual beliefs, qua
beliefs, would render the basic beliefs non-basic.

Williams expresses a somewhat similar objection in
the form of a dilemma.

Insofar as the content of immediate experience
can be expressed, the sort of awareness we have
in our apprehension of the given is just another

> type of perceptual judgement and hence is no
> longer contact with anything which is merely
> given. But if the content of immediate exper-
> ience turns out to be ineffable or
> non-propositional, then the appeal to the given
> loses any appearance of fulfilling an explan-
> atory role in the theory of knowledge; specif-
> ically, it cannot explicate the idea that know-
> ledge rests on a perceptual foundation.[64]

It is clear that neither Newman nor Plantinga can grasp the second horn of this dilemma. As grounding basic beliefs or intuition, our immediate experience must have some doxic character that justifies its being taken to ground this basic belief or intuition rather than another. Can Newman and Plantinga grasp the first horn? I think so. William's exposition of this horn of the dilemma is faulty. It is cast in the form of a implication and the implication simply does not hold. It does not follow from the fact that we express per- ceptual judgements that we do not have contact with anything that is merely given. Williams fails to dis- tinguish two things: (1) that something is given in immediate experience and (2) what it is that we take that something to be. The first is independent in principle of our prior beliefs and opinions; the second is not. Even then, what we take our experience to be of is not determined solely by our present noetic structure. The given element in our experience has a doxic character which, of course, can only find expression in terms of the categories of our language but which nevertheless restricts the possible lines of interpretation. That there is no non-linguistic way of talking about or referring to our immediate experience does not mean that our immediate experience is irreducibly verbal.

Summary Conclusion

In this chapter, I have examined the notions of assent, certitude and intuition. Assent and certitude were contrasted and an examination of intuition revealed it to be a kind of simple assent. Intuition has two distinguishable aspects: one generative; the other receptive aspect. These aspects, while distinguishable, are not really distinct. The first of these aspects corresponds to the second signification of natural inference as that was delineated in the first chapter. Finally, Plantinga's notion of basic beliefs was discussed so as to illuminate further the Newmanian notion of 'intuition.'

Notes

[1]I shall consider this section in Chapter Three.

[2]Grammar, p. 151.

[3]Newman means to be taken literally when he claims that assents are unconscious: "propositions pass before us and receive our assent without our consciousness." (Grammar, p. 157.)

[4]I shall argue in the fourth chapter that we can also distinguish two kinds of first principles: absolute first principles which are concomitant to intuition and relative first principles which are concomitant to natural inference(1).

[5]For the most part, Newman uses the terms ´complex´ and ´reflex´ synonymously. Later, however, ´reflex´ assent is the term applied to the second assent which is given to the first assent after a process of investigation. The whole process of assent, investigation and subsequent assent is now called ´complex´ assent, i.e. the primary and secondary assents taken together.

[6]Grammar, p. 162.

[7]See McCarthy on perception and inference, pp. 135-150; 165-169.

[8]See McCarthy´s three definitions of certitude, below pp. 125-126.

[9]As Ferreira notes, what Newman requires for certainty is the absence of reasonable doubt, not the absence of all possibility of doubt. See Ferreira pp. 87-97; 106-113.

[10]Grammar, p. 164.

[11]Achaval and Holmes, p. 126.

[12]Grammar, p. 168.

[13]Grammar, p. 175.

144

[14]Ferreira notes that it cannot be denied that
Newman makes conflicting claims in regard to the inde-
fectibilty of certitude.
His zeal carried him at times into two false
equations; (1) the equation of justified certitude with correct certitude, and (2) the equation of the state of an individual's mind with
the normative object, truth. In the very same
chapters that he makes these claims, however, he
denies them as well. Both in these chapters and
in scattered correspondence Newman recognizes
that certitudes fail and that men make mistakes
in their certitudes; he recognizes the distinction between the truth which cannot fail and
certitudes which can fail, and he continually
qualifies the claim to indefectibility ('on the
whole', 'as a general rule', etc.). (p. 105)

[15]Grammar, p. 181.

[16]Grammar, p. 182.

[17]Grammar, p. 189.

[18]In the fourth chapter we shall see this problem
recur in regard to first principles.

[19]This creates a problem in regard to first principles. I hold that first principles are a kind of
simple assent. I also hold that there are no explicit
rational grounds for simple assents qua intuitions,
though there are virtual rational grounds. So, first
principles, as well as prejudices, are prior to rational grounds. How then are they to be distinguished
from prejudices? Perhaps Newman should have kept the
Present Position of Catholics definition of prejudice
as not being simply prior to reason but as being
actively against it. J.H. Newman, Lectures on the
Present Position of Catholics in England, (London,
1903). Hereafter referred to as 'Catholics.'

[20]Ferreira claims (and I think he is correct in so doing) that Newman was concerned not with denying the reversibility of assents so much as with denying a certain mode of reversibility, namely a piecemeal one. The denial of change in a particular manner (namely the weakening of our unconditional acceptance by degrees) is not an all-out denial of the possibility of any change. We can finally reverse our assents, but we should do so only after maintaining a particular kind of adherence in the meantime...our assent does not vary directly with the ups and downs of inferential warrants. (85)

[21]Grammar, pp. 66-67.

[22]Newman elsewhere shows that he is not commited to a rigid faculty psychology by speaking of these faculties as ´modes´ of the minds. Grammar. p. 45.

[23]Notebooks, pp. 31-35.

[24]McCarthy, p. 161; pp. 160-164.

[25]Grammar, p. 67.

[26]Grammar, pp. 210-211.

[27]W.G. Ward, On Nature and Grace (London, 1860). Newman had received a copy of this from Ward before publication.

[28]Ward, p. 14.

[29]Notebooks, p. 35.

[30]Notebooks, p. 75.

[31]Notebooks, pp. 36-37.

[32]See the citation from the Grammar, pp. 13-14 above.

146

[33]There is an interesting debate as to whether Descartes's Cogito embodies an inference or an intuition. See Jaakko Hintikka, "Cogito Ergo Sum, Inference or Performance?" The Philosophical Review, LXXI (1962), 3-32; Jaakko Hintikka, "Cogito Ergo Sum as an Inference and a Performance,"" The Philosophical Review, LXXII (1963), 487-496; Julius R. Weinberg, "Cogito Ergo Sum: Some Reflections on Mr. Hintikka's article," The Philosophical Review, LXXI (1962), 483-491; James D. Carney, "Cogito Ergo Sum and Sum Res Cogitans," The Philosophical Review, LXXI (1962), 492-496; Harry G. Frankfurt, "Descartes Discussion of His Existence in the Second Meditation," The Philosophical Review, LXXV (1966), 329-356; Harry G. Frankfurt, Demons, Dreamers and Madmen, (New York 1970).

[34]Notebooks, p. 41.

[35]Notebooks, p. 37.

[36]"Assent and Intuition," (1860) in Achaval and Holmes, pp. 63-80.

[37]Achaval and Holmes, pp. 71-72.

[38]The difference between intuition and contuition (inference) seems to be, as Newman puts it in regard to the difference between inference and assent in the Grammar, one in the order of viewing.

[39]McCarthy, p. 139.

[40]Achaval and Holmes, p. 67. This argument is taken from Aristotle. See below, pp. 152-157. McCarthy wants to dismiss this as too problematic. I'm not so sure we can dispense with it so quickly. However, it is one thing to require proof, it is another thing not to admit of it at all. Also, it is not at all clear that the premisses have to be self-evident, i.e. possess some phenomenological characteristic which renders them luminous to the intellect. This topic will have to await a full discussion until chapter four.

[41]"On Certainty, Intuition, and the Conceivable," in Achaval and Holmes, pp. 92-119.

[42]This is a hint that there may be different classes of first principles. See chapter four below on absolute and relative first principles.

[43]Achaval and Holmes, p. 70.

[44]From chapter 17 of Cook's Account of the Voyages. Cited in Achaval and Holmes, p. 71.

[45]Achaval and Holmes, p. 71.

[46]Achaval and Holmes, p. 75.

[47]"Faculty of Abstraction", in Notebooks pp. 9-21.

[48]Almost alone among Newman's commentators, McCarthy notes the connection between Newman on perception and Newman on reasoning. He adverts to the frequency of perceptual imagery in Newman's discussion of reasoning. According to McCarthy, it is this perceptual imagery which lies at the heart of the unconscious and personal aspects of non-formal reasoning. Such reasoning is unconscious because the previous experience in which we situate the new experience, is not consciously remembered. Such reasoning is personal because what we see is (at least partially) constituted by our particular past experience. McCarthy, pp. 164-182.

[49]J.H. Newman, The Idea of a University (New York, 1959), p. 82. See also, the Grammar, pp. 290-294.

[50]Idea, p. 83.

[51]See the Grammar, p. 210.

[52]"Letter on Matter and Spirit" in Notebooks, pp. 199-216.

[53]Notebooks, p. 204 On the matter of the relationship of instinct to intuition, J. Artz seems to me to
get it right. He writes:
> The terms "instinct" and "intuition" seem to be
> interchangeable in Newman's terminology...Newman
> uses the terms synonymously. He even speaks of
> "this instinct or intuition."...Perhaps it is
> more correct to look for a distinction in the
> different function each performs in spontaneous
> knowledge rather than in the object as general
> or individual....Instinct...is a power, a prin-
> ciple of action. In contrast, intuition serves
> as a pure act of vision. If instinct is the
> leader, intuition is perhaps the goal. If they
> are not distinct in act, they are so in essence.

J. Artz, "Newman and Intuition," Philosophy Today, 1
(1957), 10-16. Given the Aristotelian source of much
of Newman's thought, this seems to me the most plausible interpretation of the distinction between instinct
and intuition. Instinct is a kind of agent or active
intellect; intuition is a kind of passive intellect.
Artz goes on to deny, as I do, that this intuition is a
priori. "With Newman, spontaneous knowledge is always
a posteriori; intuition, a seeing through the facts of
experience." (p. 12). See also Ferreira, p. 73.

[54]"Foundations of Thought," Notebooks, pp. 93-100.

[55]"Elements of Thought," Notebooks, pp. 23-29.

[56]Notebooks, p. 23.

[57]McCarthy claims that our apprehension of these
ideas is neither immediate nor intuitive but rather,
reflective. (134) But Newman has clearly shown that he
does not consider it necessary for something to be an
intuition that it be immediate. So, McCarthy's distinction between 'intuitive' ideas and 'reflective'
ideas comes to nothing.

[58]The constituents of this tension are what M. Williams, following C. I. Lewis, calls the "two components view." In knowledge, there are two components: (1) immediate data, and (2) the constructive or interpretive activity of the mind. Without the first, our knowledge is contentess and arbitrary; without the second thought is superfluous and error inexplicable. Michael Williams, Groundless Belief, (New Haven, Connecticut, 1977).

[59]Alvin Plantinga, "Reason and Belief in God," Unpublished Paper, (Notre Dame, 1981).

[60]However, even though our experiences are not expressed propositionally, still, they are proponibles, i.e. they are, indeed have to be, capable. of being expressed propositionally. We can further distinguish between first-person justification and third-person justification. In first person justification, the ground of my basic belief remains unexpressed; in third person justification, it has to be expressed. It may have been considerations such as this that led McCarthy to think of intuition and contuition (inference) as not being properly separable. McCarthy, p. 135.

[61]Plantinga makes this concession on p. 83.

[62]Plantinga, p. 87.

[63]There is a virtual or tacit belief to this effect such that, if asked whether I believed that I was being thus appeared to, I would reply affirmatively.

[64]Williams, p. 93.

CHAPTER 3

A CHANGE IN THE ORDER OF VIEWING: INFERENCE AND ASSENT

> The objective fact then which, viewed as a sub-
> ject of conviction, is relative to premisses,
> and in the luminousness of its proof, or what is
> called, evidence, when viewed as a subject of
> certainty, stands absolute and as a first prin-
> ciple and a starting point, as if with an axiom-
> atic force thus changed indeed in the order of
> viewing it (its aspect) but the same in this,
> that it is simply perceived by the mind.[1]

Newman on Inference and Assent

Now it is time to focus on the relationship bet-

ween inference and assent. Newman's problem (as he

sees it) is this. Inference is ordinarily the

antecedent of assent.[2] How is it that a conditional

acceptance of a proposition (inference) is able to lead

to an unconditional acceptance of a proposition (as-

sent)? How is it that propositions which are at most

verisimilitudinal can claim our unqualified adhesion? The whole of the second part of the Grammar is structured to reflect Newman's concern with this question. In chapters six and seven he explains what assent is; in chapter eight he deals with inference, and finally he solves "the apparent inconsistency which is involved in holding that an unconditional acceptance of a proposition can be the result of its conditional verification."[3] In the foregoing discussions I have already given the gist of chapters six, seven, and eight, but I have deliberately prescinded from considering the question of the relationship of inference to assent until now. I now propose to reconsider these chapters to discover what Newman has to say on this matter. I will present some critical interpretations of Newman's account and attempt to sift the truth from the error in them.

Why did Newman think this task of distinguishing inference from assent was important? Does it really matter if assent cannot be distinguished from inference? For Newman, it matters very much. Here is why:

> The authors to whom I refer wish to maintain that there are degrees of assent, and that, as the reasons for a proposition are strong or weak, so is the assent. It follows from this that absolute assent has no legitimate exercise

except as ratifying acts of intuition or demonstration. What is thus brought home to us is indeed to be accepted unconditionally, but, as to reasoning in concrete matters, they are never more than probabilities, and the probability in each conclusion which we draw is the measure of our assent to that conclusion. Thus, assent becomes a kind of necessary shadow, following upon inference, which is the substance, and is never without some alloy of doubt, because inference in the concrete never reaches more than probability.[4]

Let us look carefully at this passage. We have, according to Newman, two words in our vocabularies; ´inference´, and ´assent´. They refer either to the same mental act or to different mental acts: "either assent is intrinsically different from inference, or the sooner we get rid of the word in philosophy the better."[5] Some people want to maintain a doctrine of degrees of assent in which assents are directly proportional to the prior inference which elicited them. Newman´s point then is that such a picture of assent makes it a shadow of inference, and hence, redundant. Another point is this: if assent has degrees, then it has a highest degree. But assents of this degree can only be given in the presence of inferences of a correspondingly exalted status such as intuition or demonstration. Unfortunately, reasoning in concrete matters is always only probable and so it follows that

absolute assent can never be warranted here.[6] Here then
is another hint as to what ´conditionality´ consists
in. We have already seen that it means being dependent
on premisses in some way. Now we see that it is to be
equivalent to "having degrees."[7] Are these two
characteristics of the difference between inference and
assent independent or incompatible? I do not think so.
In fact, they are not only compatible, they are intrinsically related. Having degrees, or being variable, is
a simple corollary of a proposition´s being inferentially related to other propositions. I mention this
point here only to leave it. It will come up for discussion when I deal with Steinberg´s critical account
of the distinction.

The pretentious axiom that Newman is concerned to
contest goes as follows:

> [P]robable reasoning can never lead to
> certitude...assent cannot rise higher than its
> source; inference in such matters is at best
> conditional, therefore assent is conditional
> also.[8]

Newman´s attack on this ´pretentious axiom´ is twofold.
First he argues that it flies in the face of what by
all accounts is a reasonable activity of human beings.
Second, he shows that there is, in fact, no strict pro-

portional connection between inference and assent and thus, that they really are distinct. With regard to the first point we may be brief.

Newman points out that there are many propositions which everyone accepts unconditionally and which are, by their very nature, indemonstrable. Many instances of such beliefs were listed in the first chapter in the section on informal inference and so I shall not rehearse them here.

With regard to the second point, Newman asks if there is in fact such an act of the mind as assent, and, if there is, whether it is distinct from other acts?

> [I]f assent is a sort of reproduction and double of an act of inference, if when inference determines that a proposition is somewhat, or not a little, or a great deal, or very like truth, assent as its natural and normal counterpart says that it _is_ somewhat, or not a little, or a great deal, or very like truth, then I do not see what we mean by saying, or why we say at all, that there is any such act....When I assent, I am supposed, it seems, to do precisely what I do when I infer, or rather not quite so much, but something which is included in inferring; for, while the disposition of my mind towards a given proposition is identical in assent and in inference, I merely drop the thought of the premisses when I assent, though not their influence on the proposition inferred.[9]

This is a crucial passage. It will be especially important to determine the precise meaning of the last few sentences. Newman is giving expression to a position which he holds to be untenable but it is not, however, immediately clear just what it is in this passage he intends to deny.

Newman's attempt to show inference and assent to be distinct proceeds by way of what we might call the Method of Incomcomitant Variation:

1. Assents may endure without the presence of the inferential acts upon which they were originally elicited.

> [W]hen we first admitted them, [assents we had some kind of reason...for doing so. However, whatever those reasons were, even if we ever realized them, we have long forgotten them. Whether it was the authority of others, or our own observation. or our reading. or our reflections, which became the warrant of our assent, any how we received the matters in question into our minds as true, and gave them a place there. We assented to them, and we still assent, though we have forgotten what the warrant was. At present, they are self-sustained in our minds, and have been so for long years; they are in no sense conclusions; they imply no process of thought.

2. Assent can fail while the inferential act is still present.

> Our reasons may seem to us as strong as ever, yet they do not secure our assent. Our beliefs, founded on them, were and are not; we cannot perhaps tell when they went; we may have

thought that we still held them, till something
happened to call our attention to the state of
our minds, and then we found out that our assent
had become an assertion.

3. Sometimes assent is not given despite the presence
of strong and convincing arguments.

We sometimes find men loud in their admiration
of truths which they never profess....men may
believe without practising...it not unfrequently
happens, that while the keenness of the ratiocinative faculty enables a man to see the ultimate result of a complicated problem in a moment,
it takes years for him to embrace it as a truth,
and to recognize it as an item in the circle of
his knowledge.

4. We do not assent a little in proportion to the
available arguments. We either assent or we do not.

[V]ery numerous are the cases, in which good
arguments, and really good as far as they go,
and confessed by us to be good, nevertheless are
not strong enough to incline our minds ever so
little to the conclusion at which they they
point.

5. Moral dispositions can hinder assent to logically
unimpeachable conclusions.

[P]rejudice hinders assent to the most incontrovertible proofs...."A man convinced against his
will, Is of the same opinion still."

6. Even demonstrative argument is not always able to
command assent.[10]

Certainly, one cannot conceive a man having before him the series of conditions and truths on

which it depends that the three angles of a tri-
angle are together equal to two right angles,
and yet not assenting to that proposition. Were
all propositions as plain, though assent would
not in consequence be the same act as inference,
yet it would certainly follow immediately upon
it....But I am not speaking of short and lucid
demonstrations; but of long and intricate
mathematical investigations; and in that case,
though every step may be indisputable, it still
requires a specially sustained attention and an
effort of memory to have in the mind all at once
all the steps of the proof, with their bearings
on each other, and the antecedents which they
severally involve; and these conditions of the
inference may interfere with the promptness of
our assent.

Now, it is important to note that while Newman is

arguing that inference and assent are distinct, he is

not arguing that they are totally unrelated. He is at

pains to point out that, first, arguments adverse to a

conclusion naturally hinder assent; second, the _in-
clination_ to give assent varies according as inference

expresses strong or weak probability; and third, as-

sent always implies grounds in reason, implicit if not

explicit. In fact, Newman doubts that assent is ever

given without some preliminary which stands for a

reason.[11] Despite all this, the relationship between

inference and assent is not coercive. Assent can be

withheld in the presence of good reasons and, if given,

withdrawn while these reasons yet remain.

Both inference and assent are acceptances of a proposition. They differ in this, that while inference is conditional, assent is unconditional. Jay Newman argues that while it is a presupposition of Newman's criticism of Locke that assent is unconditional while inference is conditional, Newman never argues for this presupposition.[12] He also denies Newman's claim that he (Newman) has gone a long way towards showing how inference differs from assent. According to Jay Newman, four points immediately come to mind

1. Inference is not simply acceptance of a proposition. Inference is an inferring, not just an attitude towards a proposition which has been inferred.

2. To the extent that inference is acceptance of a proposition, it is certainly different from other modes of accepting a proposition, but its one special characteristic (if indeed it has only one) is not necessarily its "conditionality". Moreover, it is not completely clear what this "conditionality" consists in.

3. Assent and inference are not necessarily the only possible basic modes of accepting or holding a proposition. So, even if inference is conditional and there must be some unconditional mode of holding a proposition, it does not follow by a process of elimination that this unconditional mode is assent.

4. We would distinguish between assent and inference even if inference were simply a certain kind of assent.

In the discussion of the subsequent critical views it will become apparent that Jay Newman's four points are all wide of the mark.

If we could produce an example of a conditional assent then Newman's thesis would fall by the wayside. Can we produce one? It seems not. Newman is careful to point out that while it is true that assent is either given or not, with no half measures in between, it is _not_ true that assent has to be given only to categorical propositions. In fact, what are usually cited as examples of variations of assent to inferences are really examples of assent to variations in inference. An assent to a probability is as complete an assent as an assent to a truth. Variability may enter into the matter of the assent, but not into the act of assent itself.[13]

Reflex assent or certitude is the judgement of a judgement, or an assent of the intellect to an assent. It is an assent of the mind to an apprehension of a truth accompanied by a reference to the grounds or motiva of that apprehension. Since certitude is a species of assent and assent does not admit of degrees, neither does certitude. But though we cannot be more or less certain of a truth, we can be certain of it with more vigour, keenness, and directness, according to the quality of the evidentia. Newman does allow for variability in our assents but he locates this element of variability in the propositional object of the cer-titude and not in the act of the mind.

Newman gives us some examples of assent given to propositions which are, he says, non-intuitive and non-demonstrative. This seems to be a slip of the pen for although Newman claims these propositions are "short of intuition and demonstration"[14] the first ex-ample begins by saying "starting from intuition..."!

However, when he has presented these illustrative proposition, Newman adds "None of us can think or act
without the acceptance of truths not intuitive, not
demonstrative, yet sovereign."[15] Again, he appears to
deny that these propositions are intuitions. What are
we to make of this of this apparent contradiction? One
possible solution is that Newman may be using the term
´intuition´ in two distinct senses. However, this is
hardly likely given the fact that the whole discussion
occupies less than three pages in the original. The
other, more likely, possiblity is that Newman was tem-
porarily confused. Are we to go by what he says or by
the examples he gives us? I prefer to go by the examples, which fall into four broad categories:

1. Facts of consciousness: I exist; there is a
   right and a wrong; there is a good and an
   evil; there is a true and a false; there is
   a beautiful and a hideous. Also in this category are assents to facts of memory.

2. Facts external to consciousness: The world is
   a system with parts and wholes; the future is
   affected by the past.

3. Historical Facts: We have parents; the world
   has a history (i.e. it did not spring into
   being five minutes ago.

4. Personal Facts: We have assents concerning
   interpersonal relations, e.g. friendship,
   etc.

Now, the phrase "starting from intuition" is
clearly linked syntactically only to the first of these
categories. It is a problem to determine the extent to
which it is intended to refer to the other categories.
The problem is compounded when Newman comments that in
regard to the propositions in these categories we have
an immediate unhesitating hold on them all. This would
seem to make them all intuitions. The problem here is
that some of these propositions appeared in his chapters on inference as examples of inference and inferences are hardly immediate. Newman's difficulty in
classification here derives from his conflation of inference and assent in the catch-all notion of 'natural
inference.' Some of these exemplary propositions are
intuitions (as I have been using the term); still
others are the products of natural inferences in which

there <u>are</u> antecedents (unlike the case of intuition) but where we are largely unconscious of them.

Newman finally considers some colloquial expressions which might be taken as evidence contrary to his claim that assent is always absolute and unconditional. We talk of ´modified´, ´qualified,´ ´presumptive,´ or ´prima-facie´ assent. This is really assent to the antecedent plausibility of a fact, not to the fact itself. When we talk of ´half-assent´ we are referring to an inclination to assent, or an intention of assenting. Assent is an act of the mind so definite as to admit of no change but that of ceasing to be. We also hear of ´conditional assents.´ Again, conditions may enter into the matter of the assent but not into the act itself. To assent to "if this man is consumptive, his days are numbered" is as unconditional an assent as to assent to "of this consumptive patient the days are numbered." There are ´deliberative,´ ´rational,´ ´sudden,´ ´impulsive,´ and ´hesitating´ assents. These are merely circumstances of assenting, not intrinsic components of it. We hear of ´firm´ or ´weak´ assents. For example, historical events don´t command the same adherence that, say, personal events do. According to Newman, this increase or decrease of strength lies not in the assent, but in the imagination, in the manner in which we apprehend the propositions assented to.

Newman regards inference and assent as modes of viewing the same proposition under different aspects.

> A proposition may be true, yet not admit of being concluded;-it may be a conclusion and yet not a truth. To contemplate it under one aspect is not to contemplate it under another; and the two aspects may be consistent, from the very fact that they are two <u>aspects</u>.[16]

To worry about conclusiveness is to contemplate a proposition from one aspect, while to worry about truth is to contemplate it from another aspect. Because these are different aspects, albeit of the same proposition, they can be consistent. So, we may aim at inferring a proposition while all the time assenting to it, as we do when we are engaged in controversy. In fact, the motivation to investigate our assents often comes from controversial occasions.

If we aim at inferring a proposition to which we already assent that inferring will be the result of our "investigating" the proposition. Newman distinguishes very carefully between ´inquiry´ and ´investigation´.

Investigation is consistent with assent, while inquiry is not, for inquiry implies that one does not know where the truth lies and thus implies doubt. For educated minds, the investigation of their assents is both an obligation and a necessity even though there is the omnipresent danger of that investigation's leading to a reversal of the original assent. It is important to note that belief, as such, does not imply a positive resolution on the part of the believer never to abandon the belief. Rather, it implies, not an intention never to change, but an utter absence of the thought, or fear, or expectation of changing. We cannot really intend never to change that which we cannot really conceive of changing. Investigation subsequent to simple assent fulfills a law of our nature, for our first assents are often little more than prejudices. According to Newman this is so because the reasoning which precedes and accompanies them do not rise up to the importance of the assents themselves.[17] If we change our assents it is because of the accumulating force of the arguments which bear on the received propositions. Objections do not tell directly on assent, but when they multiply they tell against the implicit reasons or formal inferences which are its warrant and suspends its (assent's) acts and gradually undermines its (assent's) habit. Let us turn now to consider some critical discussions of Newman's inference/assent distinction.

The Critics

McCarthy claims to find three definitions of certitude in Newman's works.[18]

1. S is certain that p = df.

    1. S believes p

    2. S believes, given evidence e, it would be unreasonable for him to doubt p.[19]

2. S is certain that p = df.

    1. S believes that p

    2. If there is any proposition q, such that q seems to S to discredit or contradict p, then

1. either S believes q is false, or

2. S believes that q does not really contradict or discredit p. (Grammar 164)

3. S is certain that p = df.

   1. S knows that p

   2. S knows that S knows that p. (Grammar 161-163)

According to McCarthy, definitions 1 and 2 are descriptive; definition 3 is normative. Definitions 1 and 2 are not sufficient to rule out the falsity of p since in both cases it is possible for p to be false and yet for S to be certain that p. Definition 3, of course, rules out the falsity of p. McCarthy notes, as do I, that Newman cannot utilize this third definition, i.e. he cannot move from the psychological state of certitude (the feeling of repose, etc,) to the epistemological claim that p is true. As Newman admits, it is possible to have false certitudes. What of the first and second definitions? Are they distinct? It seems to me that 2-2 follows from 1-2. If it is unreasonable for S to doubt p, given e, then the existence of a q which seems to discredit or contradict p causes us no difficulty. Since S's belief in p is, _ex hypothesi_, reasonable then either q is false or else non-applicable. The importance of these two definitions lies in that fact that, in McCarthy's estimation, Newman is attempting to move surreptitiously from the first to the second definition. This move is apparently accomplished by distinguishing between inference and assent, and by introducing the notion of the illative sense.

Although Newman is firmly on Locke's side in at least one respect, (since at least one kind of assent, viz., reflex assent, demands some prior reasoning as a necessary condition of its legitimacy) nevertheless, Newman wants to claim that although assent issues from inference it doesn't ultimately depend on it. McCarthy argues that Newman cannot have it both ways. That is, he cannot psychologically separate assent from inference, and, at the same time, succeed in separating epistemologically legitimate from epistemologically illegitimate certitudes. In McCarthy's opinion, dissociating reflex assent from its reasons (inference) will open the door to reflex assents of every conceivable kind. Severing the link between inference and assent removes the basis for a rational discrimination between certitudes. Newman gains certitude concerning propositions that are not logically certain but only at the cost of allowing anyone else to have certitudes too, some of which may well be contradictory to Newman's certitudes.

In response to McCarthy's criticism there seem to me to be at least two options. Either severing the link between inference and assent does not entail the impossibility of rationally deciding between competing certitudes, or Newman does not really cut the link between inference and assent. Since it seems clear that Newman does in fact separate inference and assent as acts of the mind we must see if it is possible to distinguish between epistemologically legitimate and epistemologically illegitimate certitudes by means of something other than inference. Putting a wedge between inference and assent simply means that inference cannot be the sole basis of certitude which is what Newman has been saying all along.[20]

The gap between inference and assent seems to be more a psychological one than a logical one. If the connection between inference and assent were a logical one then there would be some point to McCarthy's criticism. If, however, the difference is a psychological one then McCarthy's criticism is irrelevant. McCarthy cannot accept the distinction as merely a psychological one for then he sees no way that one can distinguish legitimate from illegitimate certitudes.

In McCarthy's eyes Newman makes the mistake of failing to distinguish between reasons as necessary conditions for certitude and reasons as sufficient conditions for certitude. He claims that Newman thought reasons were a sufficient condition for certitude as described in the first definition. However, if we look at Newman's papers on Faith and Certainty[21] we see that he states that certitude is created with the help of inference but not by it alone; i.e. inference is not a sufficient condition of certitude.[22] McCarthy admits that inference is not a sufficient condition for assent

in the second definition he gives of certitude but con-
tends that Newman won´t allow it to be a neccessary
condition either. This, however, is not quite accurate. Newman repeatedly says that inference is a _sine_
qua _non_ of certitude. However, he has also insisted
that certitude can be sustained in the absence of the
inference which created it. This means that, at most,
inference is a _sine qua non_ (necessary condition) for
the original _creation_ of certitude but not for its continuing existence. ´_Sine qua non_´ cannot then be taken
to be exactly equivalent to ´logically necessary condition.´ (If I may conjure up an image, inference is
like the god of the Deists who, having created assent,
leaves it and goes on its merry way. Sometimes its way
happens to be that of the assent; sometimes not. Inference is not like the God of the theists who both
creates and conserves.) In short, McCarthy claims
that, on Newman´s view, inference is both necessary and
sufficient for certitude 1, and neither necessary nor
sufficient for certitude 2. McCarthy´s argument then
continues: since certitude 1 is a necessary condition
of certitude 2, it seems Newman is committed to holding
both that inference is a necessary and sufficient condition for certitude and, at the same time, that infer-

ence is neither a sufficient nor a necessary condition for certitude. I have already mentioned that I can find no textual support for McCarthy's definition 1 in the passage McCarthy adverts to. In a passage in "Certainty of Faith"[23] (to which McCarthy does not advert) Newman does distinguish two ´degrees´ or ´aspects´ in certitude. The first aspect is absence of doubt about the conclusion, the second is absence of fear about the premisses i.e., the belief that the grounds of the argument cannot substantially fail. If we compare these two aspects or degrees of certitude to McCarthy's first and second definitions of certitude we can detect a rough correspondence: absence of doubt corresponding to definition 1, and absence of fear corresponding to definition 2. However, the important thing to note is that Newman doesn't separate his two aspects or degrees of certitude. They are distinguishable aspects of the one act of certitude. There is no question of moving from one to the other.

According to McCarthy, the second definition is important for Newman because it is on the basis of this that he argues that since inference is neither sufficient nor necessary for certitude, then there must be some faculty beyond reason able to produce it. McCarthy is right about this. However, this merely increases my suspicion of the viability of definition 1. If Newman in fact does not put forward these definitions then no sense can be made of McCarthy's claim that Newman is attempting to pass surreptitiously from the first to the second definition.

McCarthy does however detect a certain problem in Newman's thought. If first principles, as a species of assent, are such that we can be required to produce reasons for them then their foundational status is rendered problematic. If they are outside the realm of reason altogether it is difficult to see how we can rationally discriminate between them. There is an equivocation here on 'reason' which, if noted, dissipates some of the tension. In its first sense, reason means 'premiss'; in its second, it means 'reasonable' or 'rational.' Unless the rationality of a proposition is equivalent to its being derived from premisses it doesn't follow that first principles, being independent of premisses, must be irrational. Since first principles are not based on premisses it follows that we cannot discriminate between them on that basis; however, it does not follow that we cannot discriminate between them at all. How it is that we can distinguish between first principles is one of the topics of the fourth chapter and I must leave its discussion till then.

H.H. Price, commenting on Newman's distinction between inference and assent, suggests that the modern reader would expect Newman's argument to be something like "whenever we make an inference we have to assent to the premiss in order to draw the conclusion."[24] This is the crucial difference between inferring (because p, therefore q) and implying (if p, then q.) So, we would expect Newman to argue that the notion of assent is prior to the notion of inference so that inference has to be defined in terms of assent and not vice versa. But Newman in fact doesn't employ this argument. Instead, he insists over and over again that the crucial difference between inference and assent is that the first is conditional while the second is not.

Price admits that before we assent to p we pay attention to the relevant evidence but he considers that it is very strange to call this inference. We should more naturally call this procedure estimation. The results of estimation can be expressed in the form of an inference. According to Price, what the distinction between assent and inference comes down to is this: it is one thing to recognize reasons for assenting to p; another thing actually to assent to p.

> [S]ometimes assent fails, while the reasons for it and the inferential act which is the recognition of those reasons, are still present and in force.[25]

If this is what Newman´s point amounts to then it does not follow that he is right in rejecting the doctrine of degrees of assent.

Why, asks Price, is inference conditional? In modern parlance, a conditional sentence is of the form "if....then...." which is an implication, while Newman´s inference is of the form "because...therefore...." which is the form of an inference. What turns ´because´ into an ´if´ is any uncertainty about the premises. Price holds that Newman confuses implication with inference. The confusion can be seen, according to Price, in Newman´s examples:

* if this man is in a consumption, then his days are numbered.

* of this consumptive patient, the days are numbered

According to Price, Newman claims that these two expressions are equivalent but the first is clearly an implication while the second is clearly an inference.

> To assent to-"If this man is in a consumption, his days are numbered,"-is as little a conditional assent, as to assent to-"Of this consumptive patient the days are numbered,"-which, (though without the conditional form), is an equivalent proposition. In such cases, strictly speaking, the assent is given neither to antecedent nor consequent of the conditional proposition, but to their connexion, that is, to the enthymematic inferentia. If we place the condition external to the proposition, then the assent will be given to "'That his days are numbered' is conditionally true;" and of course we can assent to the conditionality of a proposition as well as to its probability.[26]

As is apparent from this passage, the equivalence of the two propositions resides in the fact that they are both the propositional objects of acts of assent. Newman stresses the difference between the form of the two propositions by keeping their content identical. The point of the contrast, then, is that even where we have the same subject-matter embodied in propositions of hypothetical and categorical form, our assent to one proposition is just as categorical and unconditional as it is to the other. While the propositional object of our assents may range from the purely categorical to the purely hypothetical, assent is, in every case, categorical. Later on in the same paragraph, Newman says, in regard to the proposition "there will be a storm soon for the mercury is falling," that we may assent to each of the elements of this sentence besides assenting to the connection between them. Here too, Newman uses the technical term ´inferentia´ to indicate the connection between antecedent and consequent in a conditional statement. Did Newman confuse himself by using ´inference´ as a translation of ´inferentia?´ I do not think so, for in this entire passage Newman is talking about assent and not about inference at all and so it is unlikely that he is confusing the conditionality of inference with the conditionality of a conditional proposition.

According to Price, Newman claims to show the conditionality of inference. How does he do so. In a sentence: "We reason when we hold this by virtue of that." But, Price asks, does this indicate conditionality? In modern usage, this indicates just the opposite! For ´hold´ must mean something like ´assert´ and the assertion of both premisses and conclusion is precisely what distinguishes an inference from an implication.

According to Price, the distinction Newman is grasping for is that between

* inferring

* thinking about inference.

Everyone infers but not everyone thinks about inference.[27] When we think about inference there is an important point which is naturally expressed in a conditional statement, i.e. the conclusion of an inference can only be drawn if we assert the premisses, or on condition that we assert the premisses. According to Price, this is the point Newman is trying to make when he claims that in reasoning "we hold this by virtue of that." But though we can talk thus conditionally about an inference it does not follow that the person doing the inferring should express his thought in a conditional statement. So, Newman has failed to distinguish between inferring, which is a first order concept, and thinking about inference, which is a second order concept. In thinking about inference we note that to gain knowledge through inference we must be in possession of some non-inferred knowledge. We can say, if we wish, that the inference is ´conditioned´ by the possession of previous knowledge but then we must go on to distinguish between ´conditioned´ and ´conditional.´ Even if we were to grant that inference is ´conditioned´ it would not follow that inference is conditional.[28] Even granting the above, a problem remains, for Newman wants to allow ´conditionality´ to admit of degrees (otherwise, there would be no danger of confusing assent with inference; no one would be tempted to think of assent as possessing degrees.) But what does it mean to say that there are degrees of conditionality (using ´conditional´ in its modern sense)? Can one conditional sentence be more or less conditional than another? It is even more strange to say, as Newman must, that one inference is more conditional than another.

What was Newman after? What distinction did he seek to grasp by using the term ´conditional´? Let us remember that Newman´s basic point is to highlight the contrast between inference and assent. According to Price, the real difference has to do with something such as doubt, or mental reservations. Newman´s view, a la Price, is that assent, if given, has to be given without doubt or mental reservations. Assent always has a ´whole-hog´ or ´neck-or-nothing´ character. By calling inference ´conditional´ Newman is indicating that it is not to be characterized in this robust fashion. Thus construed 'conditional', signifies 'attended with doubt'. The character which inference has and assent lacks is doubtfulness, dubiety.[29] But why should anyone think that 'conditional' is equivalent to 'doubtful'? Well, in the recent past it was held that the function of a conditional clause was to express doubt or questioning. Nowadays, we take its function to be the expression of an implication or an entailment.

According to Price, Newman's doctrine of the conditionality of inference comes to this: when we recognize reasons for thinking that p without as yet assenting to p, we have some degree of doubt about the proposition p. However strong the evidence, it still leaves room for doubt. Newman tries to console us by claiming that when we assent to p, all our doubts are flung to the winds.

In Price's opinion, this interpretation of the distinction solves an exegetical puzzle. Newman had stated that the doctrine he was going to criticize was the 'degrees of assent' doctrine'. What he actually criticizes is the doctrine of the conditionality of assent. If ´conditional´ is taken to be equivalent to ´attended by doubt´ then there is a connection, for doubt does admit of degrees. Price accuses Newman of failing to notice that propositions which we doubt somewhat can nevertheless be relied upon, albeit not absolutely.

Price finishes his criticism of Newman with a fine rhetorical flourish. If Newman is right in his claims, then our human condition is more miserable and more intellectually disreputable than we commonly supposed. We need to assent to propositions on less than conclusive evidence and therefore we need to assent to these propositions with less that total or unreserved self-commitment. But, according to Price, since Newman will not allow that we can do this then our situation is miserable. We are constrained to do that which we cannot do. Our situation is disreputable in that, with less than conclusive evidence, there are, seemingly, only two attitudes. Either complete suspense of judgement, or an unreasoning all-or-nothing assent. Neither of these alternatives is palatable. The first gives us no guidance to our actions and the second is unreasonable.

Price is mistaken here in his interpretation of Newman. It _is_ true that we assent on less than conclusive evidence but it is not true that we therefore assent with total or unreserved commitment, if by that is meant that we throw all caution to the wind. Price has again forgotten that while our assent must be unconditional the object of our assent, the proposition, can range from the boldest to the most cautious of statements. For example, if, given the available meteorological data, I am of the opinion that there is a probability that it will rain during the night, then I unreservedly assent, not to the proposition "it will rain during the night," but to the proposition "It will probably rain during the night." Newman takes the wind out of Price's criticism, for he does allow a degree-having attitude to proposition, in a sense, except that he locates all these ´degrees´ within the propositional object of the assent and and not in the mental act of assent itself.

The most severe criticism of Price is that he has simply mistaken Newman´s distinction between inference and assent. I.T.Ker is the one who voices this criticism most bluntly.[30] Price has claimed that the distinction between inference and assent amounts to this: in inference we recognize reasons for assenting to p; in assent, we assent to p. Now, as Ker points out, in the opening pages of the _Grammar_ Newman has expressly linked a propositional form with both inference and assent. Propositions in the conditional form express a conclusion or an inference, propositions in the cate-gorical form express assent.[31] Looking at Newman's examples we see that the conditional form is not, as one might expect "if...then..." but "...therefore...." Ker is right. To infer is not to recognize reasons for assenting but (throught the presence of the therefore) to recognize reasons for _concluding_. In the passage from Newman (cited above, p. 130) it is easy to think, as Price does, that the reasons for assent, the recog-nition of which the inferential act is, are reasons for assent _independently_ _of_ _that_ _inferential_ _act_. Of course, Newman's point is that it is the whole complex of premisses and the inferential act which is the re-cognition of the premisses as reasons for the conclusion, which is the usual antecedent and con-comitant of assent. It is also true (and Newman never denied it) that where an argument is conclusive of truth it commands our assent.

I allow then as much as this, that, when an argument is in itself and by itself conclusive of
a truth, it has by a law of our nature the same
command over our assent, or rather the truth
which it has reached has the same command, as
our senses have. Certainly our intellectual
nature is under laws, and the correlative of
ascertained truth is unreserved assent.[32]

David Pailin is one of the few people who avoids

confusing the Newmanian notion of conditionality with

the modern notion of conditionality associated with

propositions of the form "If...then....". Pailin

writes:

When Newman says that the conclusion of an argument is necessarily ´conditional´, he is not
referring to is logical status. The ´condit-
ionality´ of a conclusion does not mean that it
is hypothetical or probable. By describing a
conclusion as ´conditional´ Newman is expressing
instead the way in which we entertain a
conclusion qua conclusion. When a proposition
is held to be a valid conclusion, it is held to
be true in so far as it is implied by other true
propositions. No matter how much we may consider that it has been convincingly demonstrated, we cannot dissociate it, as a
conclusion, from those other propositions which
implied it. Thus, the ´conditionality´ of a
conclusion refers primarily to the fact that we
do not entertain it as true in its own right but
because of its dependence on other propositions
which imply it.[33]

This is as clear a statement of the difference between

conditionality a la Price and conditionality a la New-

man as one could hope to find. Pailin also rejects

Price´s notion that conditionality has something to do

with dubitability. He is firmly of the view that the conditionality of an inference consists solely in the relationship of that inference to other propositions and not in some psychological attitude of doubt or suspicion.

> Basically, however, the ´conditionality´ of a conclusion does not refer to our doubts about its conclusiveness but to the fact that whereas a proposition to which we give assent is accepted as true without any reference, conscious or unconscious, to any other proposition, a conclusion is always regarded by us in conjunction with the other propositions which imply it.... When Newman speaks of the ´conditionality´ of conclusions he is not referring to their logical relationship to other premisses, but to the way we entertain them. This ´conditionality´ is the result of our awareness that all conclusions depend on other propositions.[34]

I am substantially in agreement with Pailin´s views on this matter. However, while it is true that the meaning of ´conditionality´ for Newman is a proposition´s relation to other propositions, still it is true that because of the particular character of that relation, we may assent to p, assent to -p, or assent to some modality of p.

Pailin has other opinions which I find less acceptable, in particular, that "the actual act of assent is a leap across a logical gulf."[35] Pailin´s postulation of this ´logical gulf´ (to be overcome by a sheer act of the will) is a consequence of his accepting demonstration as the only inferential source of certitude. If this is taken to be the case, then either we are simply coerced by arguments with no choice on our part, or we simply choose apart from reason altogether. Here I find myself in agreement with Ferreira who is of the opinion that we are not simply compelled to accept this dichotomy. It is not the case that we are simply coerced by reason; neither do we simply choose to believe. There is instead, a process of active recognition.

> Newman, therefore, distinguished between impersonal compulsion and personal constraint, between the compulsion of a logical deduction and the constraint of a rational evaluation.[36]

Our freedom to assent or not to assent is not mere license. Newman does not hold the position that we can believe anything we choose to believe or refrain from believing anything we choose not to believe. Assent is subject to the constraints of rationality.

Though differing from Pailin on some points, William Fey agrees with him in rejecting Price's interpretation of the inference/assent distinction.[37]

> Although Newman was sometimes ambiguous, his inference/assent distinction should not be taken merely as a distinction between "thinking about an inference" and "actually inferring," or bet-

ween an "inclination" to accept the conclusion
of an inference and actually accepting it, or
between accepting an "if-then" implication and
accepting a "because-therefore" inference.[38]

Interpretations such as these either suggest that assent is an idle repetition of inference or else that
assent is a decision to hold that a conclusion is certain because one ´feels´ confident about it. As Fey
points out (and he is in agreement with Ferreira in
this) Newman rejected both of these alternatives.
Fey´s own positive characterization of the distinction
is as follows

> The inference/assent distinction, then, is best
> expressed as a distinction between merely con-
> cluding and knowing. For example, an astronomer
> concludes from many calculations that there
> should be an unobserved planet. But he assents
> (knows) through a complex intellectual activity
> that he is sitting on a chair or that he was
> born of parents. His assent in knowledge is not
> merely a decision because he "feels" confident.
> It "cannot be given except under certain con-
> ditions," some obvious, some elusive, but which
> enable him to grasp that this is the case. In
> this sense, Newman combined inference and assent
> in the complex act of human knowledge. "Assent
> must be preceded by inferential acts" in the
> large sense, but the complex of reasons does not
> lead to assent in the way that premisses lead to
> a conclusion. The assents of objective know-
> ledge will "dispense with, discard, ignore,
> antecedents of any kind, although antecedents
> may have been a sine qua non condition of their
> being elicited." For we come to know, not just
> particular reasons and premisses which lead us
> to draw a conclusion, but through a complex
> operation we come to know that something is sim-
> ply true.[39]

I have some reservations about this way of putting the distinction. If assent is characterized as knowledge then it is difficult to see how certitude (which is a species of assent) could ever be mistaken. Of course, this problem only arises if we insist that for a proposition ´p´ to be known, it must be true.

To sum up so far: from Pailin we obtain the fact that ´conditionality´ refers to a mode of entertaining propositions in which they are held to be true, not in their own right, but in virtue of their dependence on other propositions which imply them. From Ferreira and Fey we obtain the fact that assent must not be considered as either being coerced by argument or being simply an arbitrary choice. Rather, it is subject to rational constraint. With these distinctions and clarifications in mind let us finally consider the most recent attempt to capture the essence of Newman´s crucial distinction.

Eric Steinberg has put forward the thesis that there are two bases for the distinction between inference and assent and that these bases are both independent and unconnected.[40] Steinberg gets off to a good start by rejecting the view that inference is hypothet-

ical and assent categorical. He notes that inference
is actually the acceptance of a proposition in a
particular way. He further notes that a causal or
evidential relation between acceptance of proposition P
and proposition Q is consistent with that acceptance of
proposition Q being either inference or assent. One
answer to the question of how inference and assent are
related is Pailin's, which is that it is basically a
psychological difference in the way the propositions
are entertained. Our acceptance of proposition P is an
inference or an assent depending on how we consider it
to be related to other propositions. According to
Steinberg, this is the truth but not the whole truth.
The difference between inference and assent does not
rest on physchological factors alone. To support this
claim, he refers to this passage:

> When I assent, I am supposed, it seems, to do
> precisely what I do when I infer, or rather not
> quite so much, but something which is included
> in inferring; for, while the disposition of my
> mind towards a given proposition is identical in
> assent and in inference, I merely drop the
> thought of the premisses when I assent, though
> not their influence on the proposition
> inferred.[41]

This is a very difficult passage. Newman is putting
words in his opponent's mouth and while it is obvious
that he considers this to be an incorrect account of

the relation of inference to assent, still, it is not so obvious how we are to understand any particular part of this passage. The passage as a whole is to be rejected; how each component is to be treated remains to be seen. That some parts of this passage are not meant to be jettisoned is obvious even from Steinberg's own interpretation for he holds that Pailin's psychological interpretation is correct as far as it goes and this interpretation can be derived from the passage. If the passage were simply to be negated completely, then Pailin's interpretation would be false instead of being merely inadequate. The components of this passage are;

1. In inference we retain the thought of the premisses; in assent, we do not.

2. In both assent and inference we retain the influence of the premisses.

3. Inference and assent involve the same disposition of the mind.

In my opinion the passage is to be interpreted as follows. In assent both the thought of the premisses and their influence is dropped. This 'dropping' of the thought and the influence of the premisses results from a disposition of the mind whose act assent is. Inference and assent involve different dispositions of the mind. Steinberg, correctly, notes that inference and assent involve different dispositions of the mind but he goes on to say that

> From the context in which the passage occurs, it seems that the different dispositions of the mind concern the kind of assurance or confidence one has in a given proposition.[42]

What this amounts to, then, is that part of the meaning of ´unconditional´ is ´certain´. So, according to Steinberg, in the distinction between conditional and unconditional, we have two factors: (a) the relationship to other propositions, and (b) certainty or uncertainty. On his interpretation, inference is the entertaining of a proposition vis-a-vis other propositions and is not certain, while assent is the contemplation of a proposition on its own and is certain. He cites another passage from the _Grammar_ to support this point.

> Assent is unconditional...inference is conditional, because a conclusion at least implies the assumption of premisses, and still more, because in concrete matter, on which I am engaged, demonstration is impossible.[43]

Inference is conditional for (i) I assume premisses and (ii) in concrete matters, demonstration is impossible.

(i) obviously refers to factor (a) while (ii) does not. Unfortunately Steinberg draws the wrong conclusion from this. He claims that inference is conditional because it is non-demonstrative. According to Newman, _all_ inference is conditional whether it is demonstrative or not. It is _more_ conditional (Newman´s phrase) if it is non-demonstrative. Non-demonstrability does not make an inference conditional; It makes it _more_ conditional. What does Newman mean by this? How can something be _more_ conditional? Well, all inference is conditional in that it is essentially dependent on propositions, but informal inference or non-demonstrative inference is _more_ conditional in that it is dependent on propositions which do not even strictly entail the conclusion. As such, this has nothing to do with certitude. For both demonstrative and non-demonstrative inferences can result in certitude. Steinberg is confused on this point and his confusion results from his failure to appreciate that, for Newman, probability is to be contrasted with demonstrability and not with certainty. Probability and demonstrability are concepts applicable only to inference while the concept of certainty is applicable only to assent.

From his misinterpretation of the above points, Steinberg thinks it follows that (a) relationship to propositions, and (b) certainty, are separate and independent elements in assent. He is surprised to find that Newman doesn't think so! Why doesn't Newman take these factors to be separate? Steinberg refers to one of Newman's arguments which is located in the preparatory papers for the Grammar.[44]

> [Certitude] cannot be immediately dependent on the reasons which are its antecedents, and cannot rightly be referred back to them as its producing cause. If it were the direct result of sight, or testimony, or arguments, then, as it has been gradually created by them, so might it be gradually destroyed, and each objection would weaken it according to its own force. But, as I have been saying, certitude does not admit of more or less -- but is a state of mind, definite and complete, admitting only of being and not being.[45]

Against this argument, Steinberg presents a counter-argument. Let us desire to have a complete set of Buffalo Nickels. One either has, or has not got a complete set. But whether one has or hasn't a complete set depends on all the factors that go to make one up, namely; the various coins, their mint condition, etc. Steinberg's point is that, like the set of Buffalo Nickels 'certainty' is dependent on particular reasons. Unfortunately, the analogy breaks down. Being a complete set of Buffalo Nickels is identical with there being a certain number of coins, each of which is in mint condition, etc. It is precisely Newman's point that certitude is not equivalent to the conditions in the context of which it arises. Steinberg's analogy simply begs the question. Whatever happens to one of its constituent conditions affects the set of Buffalo Nickels directly. We must remember that Newman's thesis is not that inference and assent are absolutely disconnected but rather that they are related in such a way that what happens in inference does not directly influence what happens in assent.

Steinberg now gives some positive arguments to show that (a), relationship to propositions, and (b) certainty, are independent. The first case involves a hospital patient who reflects "Since I feel pain (Q), I am not completely anesthetized (P)". P, according to Steinberg, is clearly an inference, nevertheless it is certain. Steinberg is mistaken. Insofar as P is an inference, it is either demonstrative or probable. Insofar as P is an assent, it is either a simple assent (potential certitude) or (if, as in this case, it fulfills the requirement of prior investigation) a certitude. The second argument involves the case where I entertain a nameless fear that I may have overlooked something in a paper that I am writing. I cannot give reasons for my fear. I am not, according to Steinberg, entitled to be certain that I have in fact overlooked something. So, the detachment of a proposition from other propositions, while it may be a sign of assent, cannot be its ground. This again misses the point. The object of our assent is not "I have forgotten something" but "I fear I have forgotten something." Steinberg also seems to be confusing assent with certitude so that if, by chance, we did assent to "I have forgotten something" this, being a mere assent, is not a certitude and may in fact be a prejudice. Certitude, on the other hand, as a reflex assent following upon investigation, cannot be a prejudice.

Summary Conclusion

In this chapter I have tried to show that the difference between inference and assent is basically a psychological one. While both inference and assent have the same propositional object the acts of the mind involved are different. Using a visual metaphor, Newman tries to illustrate the difference by claiming that inference is an act of the minds in which a given proposition is viewed in relation to the other propositions that are its premisses while in assent the proposition is viewed on its own. The term Newman uses to capture this change in the "order of viewing" is 'conditional.' This usage of 'conditional' must not be confused with another usage which intends to refer to propositions of the "if...then...." variety. Ultimately, inference and assent are related, not directly in some abstract logical calculus, but rather in the mind of the human subject whose mental acts they are. However, while assent is not subject to abstract logical restraints, it is nevertheless subject to the constraint of the norms of human rationality.

It will be appropriate here to sum up those elements of chapters one through three which will be pertinent to the final chapter. The first chapter concerned itself with the internal structure and operation of inference. It emerged from the discussion there, that what Newman calls natural inference covers two quite distinct acts of the mind: (1) the limiting case of

informal inference and (2) instinct/intuition. In the
discussion of assent and certitude in the second chapter, I tried to show that simple assent included intuition as a species. In this case there are no propositions prior to the assent. This, when combined
with the findings of chapter one means that natural
inference is used by Newman to cover both inference and
assent. Simple assent also results from that form of
natural inference which is the limiting case of informal inference. Here, however, there are propositions
prior to the assent; one is just not aware of them.
Discussing the relationship of inference to assent in
chapter three, I concluded that the difference was essentially psychological rather than logical. It
emerged from the discussion, as it touched upon certitude, that one of Newman´s problems is how to discriminate between epistemologically legitimate and epistemologically illegitimate certitudes. Because of the
lack of tight ´fit´ between inference and assent, inference cannot be the ultimate criterion which will
enable us to make this distinction. Can anything else
serve in this capacity? This question will be taken up
in the fourth chapter in the context of what Newman
calls first principles.

Notes

[1]"Papers of 1853," in Achaval and Holmes, pp. 14-15.

[2]This is true unequivocally only for reflex assent. That species of simple assent which I have been calling intuition is preceded by no inference.

[3]Grammar, p. 135.

[4]Grammar, p. 136.

[5]Grammar, pp. 140-141.

[6]Remember, for Newman, 'probable' is synonymous with 'non-demonstrative,' not 'uncertain.' Failure to appreciate this point can lead to exegetical problems as we shall see below when we come to consider Steinberg's criticism.

[7]According to Ferreira, 'conditionality' means two things for Newman. First, it means having degrees -- assent is 'indivisible' while inference varies in strength. Secondly, conditionality means being dependent on premisses -- assent is 'unqualified' adhesion because it is independent of its premisses in some sense. Ferreira, pp. 21-22.

[8]Grammar, p. 136.

[9]Grammar, 140.

[10]According to Ferreira, Newman's description of the "matter of fact" about the relation between assent and inference falls into two categories
> In one case we once had justifying inference even though we are no longer conscious of it....In the other case, we fail to assent or to maintain assent even when the reasons are recognized as good....What Newman succeeds in showing is that assent and inference are separable. In particular, he shows that (A) our inference is neither a sufficient cause nor a psychologically necessary sustaining condition of assent, and (B) that assent is not always as a 'matter of fact' exactly proportioned to inference. (p. 80)

This, and these previous five citations, are to be found in the Grammar, pp. 141-144.

[11]This holds unequivocally for reflex assent or certitude. But it does not hold for all cases of simple assent. Here, the grounds lie, not in reasons (i.e. explicit propositions) but rather in experience.

[12]Jay Newman, "Newman on Strength of Beliefs," pp. 135-136.

[13]Grammar, p. 152.

[14]Grammar, p. 148.

[15]Grammar, p. 150.

[16]Grammar, p. 158.

[17]I am contending that there is no real inferential process prior to many simple assents, namely, those simple assents which are intuitions. There is, however, a virtual inferential process, or the elements from which such a process could be made, but there is no actual inferential process. Newman admits as much later on when he talks about simple assent as being 'material', or 'interpretative' certitude. It follows that the resemblance of simple assent (intuition) to prejudice lies in the fact that both of them are prior to reason. I would draw the line between them by saying that, for assent, there are grounds while for prejudice there are no grounds.

[18]McCarthy, pp. 116-130. For convenience, I am eliminating the temporal qualifier on the list of definitions McCarthy gives. I do not think it makes any essential difference.

[19]The citation given to support this definition is Grammar, p. 250. I don't find any text to support this definition here.

[20]The additional factor of certitude is personal evaluation and judgement. See chapter four.

[21]Achaval and Holmes, pp. 122-126.

[22]This is typical. Nowhere in Newman's writings can I recall any passage which suggests that inference is ever a sufficient condition of assent.

[23]Achaval and Holmes, pp. 3-38.

[24]H.H.Price, Belief, (New York, 1969), p. 138.

[25]Grammar, p. 142. (Price's italics.) See below, p. 137, for my interpretation of this passage.

[26]Grammar, pp. 152-153.

[27]This way of presenting the distinction has some initial plausibility, especially in view of Newman's University Sermons where he remarks that every man reasons but not every man can give a reason. J.H. Newman, Fifteen Sermons Preached before the University of Oxford (London, 1892). (Hereafter, Sermons.) See Sermon XIII, "Implicit and Explicit Reason," paragraph 9.

[28]This effectively grants Newman's point. For Newman is not at all concerned with conditionality in Price's sense of that term. He is concerned with the ʿconditionedʾ character of the conclusions of arguments. Perhaps Newman did not express himself as precisely as he should have but Price's criticism is, given the relative unsophistication of nineteenth century logical terminology, close to being anachronistic.

[29]As we shall see, Price is not the only one to think this. However, in Newman's terminology, doubt is simply a form of assent, viz. assent to a negation. When Newman denies that assent can co-exist with doubt he is simply making the point that you cannot assent to p and -p at the same time and in the same respect.

[30]I.T.Ker, "Some Recent Critics of Newman," Religious Studies, XIII (1977), 63-71.

[31]Grammar, p. 25.

[32]Grammar, p. 144.

[33]D.A. Pailin, The Way to Faith (London, 1969), pp. 129-130.

[34]Pailin, pp. 130;139.

[35]Pailin, p. 175.

[36]Ferreira, p. 60.

[37]William Fey, Faith and Doubt, (Shepherdstown, West Virginia, 1976).

[38]Fey, p. 147.

[39]Fey, pp. 148-149.

[40]Eric Steinberg, "Newman's Distinction Between Inference and Assent," Unpublished paper, Brooklyn College of C.U.N.Y., 1983.

[41]Grammar, p. 140.

[42]Steinberg, pp. 6-7. With all due respect to Steinberg, it is not at all evident that Newman is concerned with any psychological attitude of assurance or confidence in this passage.

[43]Grammar, p. 28.

[44]Achaval and Holmes, pp. 120-139.

[45]Achaval and Holmes, pp. 123-124.

CHAPTER 4

FIRST PRINCIPLES

In this chapter, I shall apply the findings of the first three chapters to the notion of a first principle. Just as there are two natural inferences, and two simple assents corresponding to them, so also there are two kinds of first principles. We have absolute first principles, corresponding to natural inference qua instinct and simple assent qua intuition; and relative first principles, corresponding to natural inference qua limiting case of informal inference and its concomitant simple assent. The chapter begins with a glance at some central Aristotelian notions which will shed some light on Newman's account of first principles. Then we shall see that the conflation of inference and assent which we detected in natural inference resurfaces in the illative sense. This faculty appears to have two quite distinct functions, one in regard to intuition, and another in regard to inference. Having considered the views of Newman's chief critic in the matter of first principles, the book concludes with a discussion of the possibility of choosing rationally between competing sets of first principles.

Aristotle

Considering the great influence that Aristotle had on Newman it is always wise, when investigating Newman's thought on any given subject matter, to begin by looking for analogues in Aristotle. There is a trio of central concepts to be found in Newman which can also be found in Aristotle. In Newman they appear as intuition, instinct, and first principles; in Aristotle they are <u>Nous</u>, <u>Epagoge</u>, and <u>Arche</u>. Let us begin by considering Aristotle on <u>Arche</u>.

According to Aristotle, the premisses of demonstrated knowledge must be primary, i.e. they must be appropriate basic truths. A basic truth in a demonstration Aristotle calls an 'immediate proposition,' which, in turn, is defined as "a proposition which has no other proposition prior to it."[1] Aristotle considers and rejects the thesis that Newman also considers and rejects, namely, that all knowledge involves demonstration.[2] This for two reasons. First, if all knowledge is demonstrable then either we land ourselves in an infinite regress of justification, or we have a finite regress ending with propositions which, not being demonstrable, are also unknowable (<u>ex hypothesi</u>.) The conclusion we are driven to is, of course, that no scientific knowledge is possible, which, for Aristotle is a reduction to absurdity of this supposition. Second, if we hold that all knowledge involves demonstration then we can avoid the conclusion of the previous line of argument only if we hold the justificatory regress to constitute a large circle. On this view, every given proposition is demonstrable via another and no proposition is undemonstrable. Aristotle will not allow this kind of circular justification to count as demonstration. Demonstration, for Aristotle, makes use of two essential notions; ´priority´ and ´being better known than.´ Obviously, since the relationship of priority is not reciprocal, circular justification cannot encompass that notion. So too with the notion ´being better known than...´: it, also, is not reciprocal. Aristotle concludes from all of this that the foundations of knowledge are immediate truths, or basic premisses, which are indemonstrable yet knowable.[3]

The obvious question which Aristotle has to answer now is "How do these immediate truths come to be known if they are not known by demonstration?" Aristotle proceeds to consider this issue by considering four possibilities:

1. Basic premisses are known in the same way as the conclusion of a demonstration and hence, they are knowable scientifically.

2. We have scientific knowledge about the conclusion of a demonstration; do we have a different kind of knowledge of basic premisses?

3. Basic premisses are innate in us albeit unnoticed.

4. Basic premisses come to be in us in some way and so are not innate.[4]

Concerning the third point, Aristotle notes that it is surely rather odd to believe that we in fact possess apprehensions of basic premisses and fail to notice them! Remember, for Aristotle, demonstration involves passing from the intrinsically more knowable to the instrinsically less knowable. So the force of the paradox is that of our possessing innately the most immediately knowable premisses and yet being unaware of them. Concerning the fourth point, Aristotle makes this claim: if it be true that basic premisses come to be in us then how is it that we apprehend them without prior knowledge? Since basic premisses are requisite for knowledge then we would need basic premisses in order to come to know our basic premisses!

So, the third and fourth points are excluded from consideration, and we know from previous discussion that the first point is also excluded. This leaves only the second position, namely, that basic premisses are knowable in a different way from scientific knowledge. According to Aristotle, we must possess some capacity that is not in itself knowledge (or else we land in the fourth position) which will make possible the apprehension of basic premisses. What can this capacity be? By way of answer Aristotle tells us the following story.[5]

All animals have sense perception. In some animals, this sense-perception persists, in others it fails to persist. In the latter case knowledge is not possible. However, the mere persistence of sense-perception, while necessary for knowledge, is not sufficient for it. Among the animals in which sense-perception persists we find some with the power to systematize the persistent sense-perceptions and some without this power. This systematization of the persistent sense-perceptions Aristotle calls memory. From the frequent repetition provided by memory comes experience which is the universal stabilized in its entirety. The universal is present in the original singular sense-perception but it requires persistence, systematization and repetition to bring it to light. This entire process Aristotle calls induction (Epa-goge). So, the mechanism which produces basic premisses is induction.

> Thus it is clear that we must get to know the primary premisses by induction; for the method by which even sense perception implants the universal is inductive.[6]

But the question of how we know the primary premisses still remains. As we have seen, we do not know them via scientific knowledge. How then? "By intuition (Nous)" says Aristotle.

> There will be no scientific knowledge of the primary premisses, and since except intuition, nothing can be truer than scientific knowledge, it will be intuition that apprehends the primary premisses.[7]

There is a certain ambiguity in the phrase "come to know" as it occurs in the question "How do we come to know basic premisses?" In one sense of the phrase we come to know them via induction (i.e. this is the pro-cess by which they are brought before us.) The more basic sense of the term, is, however, given that we have been provided with the universal via induction, how do we recognize it? To Aristotle, there is no fur-ther level of explanation here to which we can regress. The primary premiss is so and we see it to be so.

How does all this tie in with Newman? Well, we have seen that Newman uses two terms, ´instinct´ and ´intuition.´ If we accept the Aristotelian notion of an active productive process and a passive recognition logically subsequent to that process then we can get a plausible equation between Aristotle´s Nous and Newman´s intuition, and Aristotle´s Epagoge and Newman´s instinct.

Newman uses the terms induction and abstraction to describe the process by which we move from particular experiences of material objects to the general propos-ition "There is an external world." Similarly, we operate via induction in moving from particular cases of the operation of conscience to "There is a judging and just God." Now, Newman uses the term ´instinct´ to describe a force which spontaneously impels, not only to bodily movements, but also to mental acts. It seems, then, not unreasonable to take instinct to be equivalent to Aristotle's Epagoge and intuition to be equivalent to Aristotle's Nous. Instinct is a process, and intuition is the terminus of the process.

The similarities between Newman's first principles and Aristotle's Arche are obvious. Both for Aristotle and for Newman, first principles are necessary for knowledge. For both, they are propositions which are basic and immediate. There are, however, differences. It would seem for Aristotle that basic premisses are necessarily true. This is not so for Newman. Also, for Aristotle first principles are required primarily for demonstrative knowledge. For Newman, all our knowledge, our certitudes and our assents rest on first principles. In addition, it would seem that for Aristotle, first principles are available to all who will take the trouble to look and see them. For Newman, there is a personal element in the apprehension of first principles which is irreducible and which can give rise to potentially irreconcilable conflicts.

Noetic Faculty, Prudentia, and the Illative Sense

We have seen how Aristotle called the intuitive apprehending faculty, Nous. Newman was to do likewise - but not until the year 1885! My thesis in this section is that Newman's treatment of the illative sense in the Grammar, (and his treatment of Prudentia in earlier papers) is vitiated by the conflation of intuition and inference in the notion of natural inference. Newman finally recognizes the necessity to distinguish two faculties, one corresponding to intuition, the other to inference. When we come to consider his discussions of Prudentia and the illative sense it will be seen that they both conflate the intuitive and instinctive faculties so carefully distinguished in 1885.

> There is a faculty in the mind which acts as a complement to reasoning, and as having truth for its direct object thereby secures its use for rightful purposes. This faculty, viewed in its relation to religion is, as I have before said, the moral sense, but it has a wider subject-matter than religion, and a more comprehensive office and scope, as being, the apprehension of first principles, and Aristotle has taught me to call it nous or the noetic faculty.[8]

Newman has already indicated that reasoning is primarily an instrumental faculty. As such it demands a complement. What is the sense of there being an instrument without there being someone or something to use it? So, granted that the noetic faculty makes use of reasoning, how are the two faculties connected? The answer is, of course, obvious. They are connected through the antecedent in the chain of reasoning. As great a faculty as reasoning is, yet it is dependent on other faculties for the production of its antecendents.

> In such matters the independent faculty which is
> mainly necessary for its healthy working and the
> ultimate warrant of the reasoning act, I have
> hitherto spoken of as the moral sense; but, as
> I have already said, it has a wider
> subject-matter than religion, and a larger name
> than moral sense, as including intuitions, and
> this is what Aristotle calls nous.[9]

Newman is anxious to stress the complementarity of the two faculties. He is not exalting the one at the expense of the other.

> What could be more natural, what more congruous
> that that there should be a faculty which was
> concerned with the antecedent of the reasoning,
> as the reasoning itself is concerned with the
> consequent, so that the two faculties unite in a
> joint act, each of the two having need of the
> other.[10]

Reason is rightly used when its antecedents are supplied by intuitions, dictates of conscience, the inspired Word, the decisions of the Church, etc. Reason is wrongly used when its antecedents are supplied by human affection, narrow self-interest and bad education. It is true that reasoning cannot itself find, frame or verify its antecedents. But why should this cause us concern? We have a faculty other than reason which enables us to do that. The noetic faculty is able to find, frame, and verify the antecedents of inference, viz. first principles.[11] Reason is _not_ able to find, frame, or verify its antecedents.

In his discussion of Prudentia, Newman begins by making a distinction between what he calls ´Evidentia Veritatis´ and ´Evidentia Credibilitatis.´[12] In the case of Evidentia Veritatis its premisses are generally received and its logical process is short. In the case of Evidentia Credibilitatis its premisses are recondite and personal and the logical process is intricate and indefinitely long. So, Evidentia Veritatis admits of scientific treatment and external exhibition whereas Evidentia Credibilitatis is lodged in the minds of the individual possessing it and if it admits of science at all, admits of it but partially.

What we have here in this distinction between the two sorts of Evidentia is clearly an adumbration of the later distinction between formal inference and informal inference in the Grammar.[13] The name of the faculty which sees, furnishes, uses, dispenses and applies the premisses of the _Evidentia_ _Credibilitatis_ is _Prudentia_ or Judgement. Note that _Prudentia_ ´sees´ and ´supplies´ the premisses of the various inferential processes. Then it goes on to use these premisses in inference. So, _Prudentia_ has two clearly distinguishable functions which, as we have seen above, Newman finally distinguishes as the Noetic Faculty and the Reasoning Faculty.[14] _Prudentia_ provides the premisses (first principles) which ground the informal inference in the context of which the formal inference can be found. In the case, say, of a scholarly argument concerning the authorship of a disputed text, _Prudentia_

1. detects the arguments for referring a certain book to an author

2. weighs the worth of the arguments.

3. combines and disposes of those arguments

4. combines and disposes of the objections

5. presents the arguments as one mass in a form sufficient to take their place in the minor of a syllogism.

Of these five points, the first is a function of what Newman in his 1885 paper calls the Noetic Faculty. Points two through five are a function of what he calls (in 1885) the Reasoning Faculty. In the present context they are all functions of Prudentia.

This Prudentia is partly a natural common endowment, partly a special gift, and partly the result of experience. It varies with the subject matter on which it is employed and it goes under many names: sagacity, common sense, strong sense, shrewdness, acuteness, penetration, instinctive perception, tact of experience, etc. It is Prudentia which decides which subject-matters admit of proof, which of credibility, how many and what arguments are necessary in each case to prove credibility, etc. Prudentia is really an architectonic faculty; it extends to all subjects. It is just that some matters are capable of being reduced to a science and so Prudentia is left in possession of those which are not so reducible.

Since Evidentia Credibilitatis cannot take its multifarious premisses for granted and since the form of the argument is elaborate, circuitous and perplexed, how are we to convince another by this means? Given

that we apprehend the truth of p by means of Evidentia
Credibilitatis, how are we to cause the reception of
the truth of p in others? Newman reverses the question. Given that others apprehend the truth of x by
Evidentia Credibilitatis how are we to do so? In two
ways: by ourselves gaining the Prudentia in the
particular subject matter under consideration; or by
using the Prudentia of others who are already experienced in that particular discipline. The second way
is the more common though it is really a variant of the
first, for the duty of going by the skills of others is
one of the very principles which Evidentia Credibilitatis requires and which Prudentia dictates.

Newman, throughout all this has been claiming that
Evidentia Credibilitatis is a kind of demonstration
just as much as Evidentia Veritatis. He now elaborates
just what he means by this. For him demonstration
means a valid proof, certain portions of which can be
drawn out scientifically. It is also demonstrative in
that anyone who studies its premisses fairly will find
the proof irresistible. The demonstrability of Evidentia Credibilitatis does not mean that it can be forced
on the mind of anyone whatever who understands argument

by a process of logical formulae such as would be the case in a demonstration of Euclid. Ferreira's distinction between logical compulsion and rational constraint is applicable here. Whatever be the case with _Evidentia Veritatis_, it is clearly the case that what we are dealing with in the case of _Evidentia Credibilitatis_, when Newman talks about demonstration, is not logical compulsion but rational constraint.[15]

In his discussion of the illative sense in the _Grammar_, Newman begins by noting that some people argue that, since experience can lead only to probabilities, certitude is always a mistake. Others, accepting the principle but rejecting the conclusion, argue that, since we are entitled to be certain and since experience leads only to probability, we must therefore have recourse to intuitions to justify our certitudes. Newman denies the principle common to both parties to the argument: it just is not true that probabilities can never lead to certitude. In support of this claim, it is enough to appeal to the common voice of mankind: "That is a law of our mind which is exemplified in action on a large scale, whether _a priori_ it ought to be a law or no."[16] According to Newman, reason never bids us to be certain except on an absolute proof and such a proof can never be furnished by the logic of words, for, as certitude is of the mind, so is the act of inference which leads to it.

Newman asks the following question. "Is there any criterion of the accuracy of an inference such as may be our warrant that certitude is rightly elicited?" He answers "The sole and final judgement on the validity of an inference in concrete matter is committed to the personal action of the ratiocinative faculty, the perfection or virtue of which I have called the Illative Sense."[17] It is clear that Newman has not made any advance on the Papers of 1853. The illative sense is still the perfection of the ratiocinative faculty. As we shall see below when Newman comes to deal with first principles, the same confusion of function permeates these as permeates Prudentia and the illative sense.

The Illative Sense derives its sanction from the fact that we are beings with a certain, nature, certain faculties, existing in a particular world with definite characteristics. I will let Newman talk for himself:

> We are in a word of facts; we use them [our faculties], for there is nothing else to do...We are conscious of the objects of external nature and this consciousness, reflection, and action

we call our rationality...Our being, with its
faculties, mind and body, is a fact not admitting of question, all things being of necessity
referred to it, not it to other things...There
is no medium between using my faculties, as I
have them and flinging myself upon the external
world according to the random impulse of the
moment...I am what I am, or I am nothing. I
cannot think, reflect, or judge about my being
without starting from the very point which I aim
at concluding. My ideas are all assumptions,
and I am ever moving in a circle...My first elementary lesson of duty is that of resignation to
the laws of my nature.[18]

Man is born with a certain nature but his progress and

his perfection lies in his own hands. This progress is

neither necessary nor mechanical and it is dependent on

our personal efforts. This progress is carried out by

the acquisition of knowledge of which inference and

assent are the immediate instruments.

[I]nstead of devising, what cannot be, some sufficient science of reasoning which may compel
certitude in concrete...confess that there is no
ultimate test of truth besides the testimony
born to truth by the mind itself, and that this
phenomenon, perplexing as we may find it, is a
normal and inevitable characteristic of the mental constitution of a being like man. His progress is a living growth, not a mechanism; and
its instruments are mental acts, not the for-
mulas and contrivances of language.[19]

The use of the illative sense is illustrated by refer-

ence to parallel faculties. For example, in moral

matters, there may be rules, but the application of

those rules to concrete matters is left to the indiv-

idual. The illative sense comes of an acquired habit
(though it originates in nature) and is formed and mat-
ured by practice and experience. The law of truth differs from the law of duty for, whereas the law of duty
changes, the law of truth never changes. However, even
though truth is ever one and the same, the reasonings
which carry us to truth and certitude are many and
varied and differ from inquirer to inquirer. In the
case of the fine arts rules may be given but only some
have the capacity to embody them in their works. In
the practical arts, skill is a sort of instinct, not an
obedience to external rules of criticism. The relationship which exists in all these cases is similar
to that which exists between the illative sense and
reasoning.

The illative sense has four distinct aspects:

1. It is one and the same in all concrete mat-
    ters, though employed in them in different
    measures. We do not reason one way in chem-
    istry and another way in religion. We proceed
    as far as possible by the logic of language
    and we are obliged to supplement it by a more
    subtle and elastic logic of truth.

2. It is attached to definite subject-matters.

3. The mode of reasoning of the illative sense is the same in all fields. It is the elementary principle of modern mathematics, namely, approximation to a limit,

4. It is the ultimate test of truth and error in our inferences (as other mental senses are to other subject matters.)

The illative sense works in the beginning, middle and end of inquiry.[20] Reasoning in language is a valuable tool for achieving the ends of our inquiries but for all its usefulness, it is only a work of the mind. And as that which creates is superior to its creation, so the mind is more vigorous and versatile than any of its works. Only by the exercise of mind does the margin disappear that intervenes between verbal argumentation and conclusions in the concrete. It determines what science cannot, namely, the limit of converging probabilities and the reasons sufficient for a proof.

In the middle of inquiry, it is not by any diagram
that we are able to scrutinize, sort, and combine the
many premisses. It is the living mind which uses the
principles, facts, doctrines, experiences, and testim-
onies.

In the beginning of the inquiry, the action of the
mind is necessary to ascertain the first elements of
thought, the assumptions, principles, tastes and opinions which are half the battle in finding the
conclusion with which the reasoning is to terminate.

> It is the mind itself that detects them in their
> obscure recesses, illustrates them, establishes
> them, eliminates them, resolves them into sim-
> pler ideas as the case may be. The mind contem-
> plates them without the use of words, by a pro-
> cess which cannot be analyzed.[21]

This is clearly intuition, as the sentence I have italicized shows. However, a little further on, Newman
attributes this process of intuitive contemplation to
the illative sense, the architectonic faculty of reasoning!

> [T]he illative sense has to act [on these ele-
> mentary contrarieties of opinion], discovering
> them, following them out, defending or resisting
> them, as the case may be.[22]

Newman is confusing the issue. As will become obvious
from our discussion of first principles, the illative

sense, as the architectonic faculty of reasoning cannot be involved in their detection. All this confusion results ultimately from Newman's inability to get clear on the difference between intuition and inference and his conflation of the two notions in natural inference.

One drawback of the illative sense is that it provides no common measure between mind and mind. The ratiocinative talent, of which the illative sense is the perfection, can, in disputed cases, merely point out where the differences lie between A and B, how far they are immaterial, and whether it is worth while continuing the argument. This is so because all reasoning is from premisses and these premisses arise in their first elements from personal characteristics in which men are in essential and irremediable variance with one another.

The use of the illative sense in the end of inquiry has already been illustrated in the discussion of informal inference. It remains to examine its role in more detail in the beginning and middle of inquiry.

Let us begin in media res. Here are some of the questions that have to be resolved in considering some historical matter. Where shall I start, given the presence of received accounts? What will be my point of view? What are the principles to be used? What opinions can be set aside as nugatory? What arguments are to be considered apposite? What are the false issues to be avoided? Should I disregard everything hitherto received? - retain it in outline? - make selections from it? - interpret it as mythical or allegorical? How far are tradition, analogy, isolated monuments, ruins, vague reports, legends, popular proverbs, etc., to tell in my inquiry? What are the marks of truth? - falsehood? - probability? Can any conclusion be given to the argument? - a probable conclusion? - a certain conclusion? In order to answer these questions we must use our judgement and how we use our judgement depends on our intellectual complexion.

To illustrate his point Newman gives a succinct account of the Niebuhr, Clinton, Mure and Gorte, Lewis, controversy on the history of Rome. Why do these authorities differ from each other so much? Because their estimates are their own and come from their own particular judgements. These judgements issue from assumptions that are peculiarly their own and they arise out of the state of their thought. Niebuhr, for example, adopts this as a working principle: no evidence is to be approved which has not first proved its right to be admitted; where there is insufficient evidence there should be no belief. Clinton acknowledges as real persons all those whom there is no positive reason for rejecting. He puts the onus of proof on those who would impugn received facts. Gote and Lewis put the onus of proof on those who defend received accounts, and More advises that reasonable indulgence be accorded to popular belief and that we defer to ancient history. According to Newman, it is tacit understanding of the vague and impalpable notions of ´reasonableness´ which makes conclusions possible. The conclusions vary with particular writers for each writes from his own point of view and with his own principles and these points of view and principles admit of no common measure.

> Men become personal when logic fails; it is their mode of appealing to their own primary elements of thought, and their own illative sense against the principles and judgement of another.[23]

We may conclude from Newman´s example that the function

of the illative sense in the middle of inquiry is to articulate and arrange sets of propositions that are consistent with our first principles. Now let us turn to the role of the illative sense in the beginning of inquiry.

The statement of the case in any particular matter depends on the particular aspect under which we view the subject. For example, in Newman's opinion, the sciences are <u>suggested</u> by nature but created by the mind. One aspect of viewing nature suggests the system of final causes. Another aspect suggests the system of efficient causes. The illative sense underlies our ability to detect the principles at the base of a heap of facts. Some principles are unreal, or over-ingenious, e.g. philosophical views of history where there is little or nothing corresponding to reality. In philosophical history there is little or nothing suggested by nature; everything is supplied by the mind. These points of view are intensely personal. Where more than one point of view is possible we hold only one. If physical objects admit of being variously apprehended, so much more do mental objects admit of diverse apprehensions.[24]

According to Newman, it is not a disproof of objective truth to find that not all men are in possession of it but it does suggest that there is something deeper in our differences than accidents or external circumstances. In the beginning of an argument we choose some propositions and exclude others. We must have the right to thus select otherwise we should be inundated with nonsense. This right to make assumptions is sometimes disputed. This is absurd if it is the general capacity which is being called into question. It is acceptable if only particular assumptions are being called into question.

If asked to choose between the principles of the sceptic or the principles of the believer, Newman says:

> I would rather have to maintain that we ought to begin with believing everything that is offered to our acceptance, than it is our duty to doubt of everything.[25]

Newman gives us some examples of the conflict of first principles. Ought government and legislation be of a religious character or not? Do magistrates exercise a retributive or a corrective office? Is Scripture or the Rule of Faith to be our ultimate guide in religious matters?

Among the factors by which a question is to be decided are antecedent reasons. These are in great measure made by ourselves and they belong to our personal character. Antecedent reasoning, when negative, is safe: e.g. a good character goes far in destroying the force of even reasonable charges. Antecedent reasoning is used by all. Unbelievers use it from the order of nature against the possibility of miracles. If this is meant to establish antecedent improbability then we have no objection. If it is meant to imply impossibility then they are guilty of using a presumption as if it were a proof.

Our discussion of the illative sense, _Prudentia_ and the Noetic Faculty has revealed how Newman's initial conflation of intuition and inference has permeated his characterisation of the architectonic faculty of reasoning. As _Prudentia_ and illative sense, the faculty is made to do double duty. Only in 1885 does Newman finally recognize that these duties involve faculties which, while complementary, are distinct. One of these faculties is concerned with the regulation of our inferential processes; the other is concerned with the establishment of the initial premisses to be

used in those inferential processes. This establishment of primary premisses is not itself a function of
our reasoning faculty and so does not, strictly speaking, fall under the jurisdiction of the illative sense.
As the architectonic faculty of reasoning, the illative
sense functions legitimately in the beginning and
middle of inquiry; it has no place in its beginnings.

First Principles

Newman's earliest attempt at sketching a theory of
first principles comes in his lectures on The Present
Position of Catholics in England delivered in 1851.[26]
These lectures occured in a polemical context and
Newman's interest was not so much in first principles
per se as in the help they could give him when applied
to controversial religious matters. His task was to
defend Catholicism against prejudice and bigotry and to
that end he found it necessary to distinguish these
attitudes from first principles. The Catholics account
is a rough sketch and it would be a mistake to take it
as embodying a fully articulated position. On the
other hand, the problem of adjudicating rationally bet-

ween disputants who possessed contradictory sets of first principles was a perennial problem for Newman. In Catholics we have displayed embryonically those elements in Newman's thought which were to provide the elements for his mature thought on the matter.

There are beliefs/opinions which do not rest on previous grounds, are not drawn from facts for which no reason can be given (or no sufficient reasons), which proceed immediately from the mind and which the holder considers to be, as it were, part of himself; if challenged, the holder cannot say "I will reconsider my reasons" for he has no reasons to consider.[27] Can anything make a person abandon such beliefs, if he holds them and continues to hold them, whatever is urged to the contrary? It seems not. Are these beliefs then prejudices? No; because prejudices are opinions formed upon grounds which the holder refuses to examine whereas these beliefs and opinions have no grounds at all.[28] The contrast between first principles and prejudices is this: first principles have no grounds, they are assumed. They cannot be proved, being, as they are, the means of proof; prejudices have grounds which the holder of the prejudice chooses to ignore.

They are beliefs held against (not prior to) reason.
They are simply persuasions or sentiments which he cannot help holding and which come to him inexplicably.
These are first principles. For example "All blacks
are unintellectual" is a prejudice if held against the
facts, whereas "God cannot punish in hell" is a first
principle because it hardly comes within the reach of
the facts at all. Newman is emphatic that first principles may be either false or true: indeed he claims
that this is the very point he intends to make.

> From what I have said, it is plain that First
> Principles may be false or true; indeed, this
> is my very point, as you will presently see.
> Certainly, they are not necessarily true; and
> again, certainly there are ways of unlearning
> them when they are false.[29]

But are there, in fact, any such things as first principles?

> Now that there must be such things as First
> Principles -- that is, opinions which are held
> without proof as if self-evident, -- and, more-
> over, that every one must have some or other,
> who thinks at all, is evident from the nature of
> the case.[30]

If you trace back your reasons for an opinion you must
stop somewhere. Since the regress cannot go on forever
what one eventually arrives at is something that cannot
be proved and that is a first principle.[31]

Why must everybody have some first principles? Because even the sceptic has to have a first principle, viz., "nothing can be known for certain." This is itself a prime example of a first principle. To illustrate the regress process involved in the arrival at first principles. Newman gives this example:

* Q: Why do you ignore S?
* A: Because S belongs to party Y.
* Q: What's wrong with party Y?
* A: Their principle is to stand upon their own rights.
* Q: What is wrong with that?
* A: It is selfish and proud.
* Q: What is wrong with selfishness and pride?
* A: It is the sin of the fallen angels.

It is somewhat difficult to say where precisely the first principle lies here; I am sure it could be formulated in many different ways, the basic point being, I take it, that selfishness and pride are, as it were, self-evident moral evils. Newman is not sparing with his examples of first principles. Here are some more:

* Man is a social being.

* A man may defend himself.

* Man is responsible.

* Man is frail and imperfect.

* Reason must rule passion.

* There is no evil so great as humiliation.

* Whatever nature requires is to be done.

* We have absolute control over, and no duties

  towards, animals.

First principles have several characteristics. They are the means of proof; they are not themselves proved.[32] First principles are like absolute monarchs; if true, they are like good and wise fathers; if false, they are like cruel and baneful tyrants.

> They are our guides and standards in spec-
> ulating, reasoning, judging, deliberating, de-
> ciding, and acting; they are to the mind what
> the circulation of the blood and the various
> functions of our animal organs are to the body.
> They are the conditions of our mental life; by
> them we form our view of events, of deeds, of
> persons, of lines of conduct, of moral qual-
> ities, of religions. They constitute the diff-
> erence between man and man; they characterize
> him. As determined by his First Principles,
> such is his religion, his creed, his worship,
> his political party, his character, except as
> far as adventitious circumstances interfere with
> their due and accurate development; they are,
> in short, the man.[33]

Does Newman adhere to this comprehensive vision of the role and function of first principles throughout his writings? I am inclined to answer this question affirmatively. This emphasis on the personal and deep-rooted nature of the Illative Sense is also found in the Grammar[34] which is Newman's most mature work.

We can easily see that first principles have these characteristics if we observe the participants in a conversation. Abel and Bundy converse on a topic. They do not agree. Neither makes any head way with the other but each becomes convinced of his own correctness. Why is this?

> [E]ach starts from some principle or opinion which he takes for granted, which he does not observe he is assuming, and which, even if he did, he would think too plain to speak about or attempt to prove. Each starts with a First Principle, and they differ from each other in first principles.[35]

If the topic were, let us say, Milton's status as a poet they could argue back and forth about it, but if they don't agree on first principles they will argue back and forth forever. Or to take another example: Abel and Bundy have similar religious views. In time they diverge. Abel becomes an atheist, Bundy becomes a Catholic. What happened to their original unanimity? According to Newman, what happened was that some latent first principles came into play so that, in fact, their original unanimity was more apparent than real.

There are many first principles common to the great mass of mankind and they are therefore true "as having been imprinted on the human mind by its Maker."[36] We have to be careful here not to misinterpret Newman. The universal reception of these first principles is a sign of their source, i.e., God, and it is because these first principles come from God that they are true. Newman is operating tacitly with some such syllogism as this:

* Whatever comes from God is necessarily true
* that which is universally received must come from God
* therefore, what is universally received is true.[37]

Among these universally received first principles are those concerning the great truths of the moral law, the duties of justice, truth and temperance, etc. Some first principles are individual and hence of no authority; still more are common only to particular localities and possess a limited authority.[38]

Newman does not blame people for following their first principles. On the contrary,he insists that they are morally obliged to do so. This obligation holds even when these first principles are objectively wrong. What Newman does blame others for is for forgetting that other people have first principles too and that the resolution of many vital questions hinges on this factor. "All depends on which set of principles you begin by assuming."[39] The basic question is, of course, which first principle or set of first principles is true?

Whereas prejudice is the rejection of reason altogether, bigotry is the imposition of private reason. It is the putting forward of a particular set of first principles as if they were the standard of every argument, investigation and judgement. If your first principles are true and they conflict with mine then, of course, my first principles are false. But my first principles are not false simply because your first principles are yours![40] Now, Newman is careful to note that not all ´imposition´ of first principles is bigotry. Those first principles which, like the truths of morality, are universal are such that their use by us in judging others is not bigotry.

> Bigotry is the infliction of our own unproved
> First Principles on others, and the treating
> others with scorn or hatred for not accepting
> them. There are principles, indeed, as I have
> already said, such as the First Principles of
> morals, not peculiar or proper to the individ-
> ual, but the rule of the world, because they
> come from the Author of our being, and from no
> private factory of man. It is not bigotry to
> despise intemperance, it is not bigotry to hate
> injustice or cruelty; but whatever is local, or
> national, or sectional, or personal, or novel,
> and nothing more, to make that the standard of
> judging a existing opinions, without an attempt
> at proving it to be of authority, is mere ridi-
> culous bigotry.[41]

Now if bigotry is the infliction of our _unproved_ first

principles, this is an indication that these particular

first principles must be susceptible of proof. This is

another passage which suggests strongly that there are

distinct types of first principle.

Newman is arguing in a polemical context and he

takes his examples from there. The reasons given for

the rejection of Catholic practices obtains leverage

only if based on non-Catholic principles. According to

its non-Catholic critics, Catholic ritual is mere form,

because Divine favour cannot rest on external obser-

vances; Catholic penitential practice are bondage

because there is no such thing as sin; Catholic wor-

ship is blasphemy _because_ God cannot be present in

ceremonies; Catholic prayer is mummery <u>because</u> prayer
cannot move God. The clause after each ´because´ above
expresses a principle which is not acceptable to Catholics.[42]

Newman has suggested that there are ways of unlearning first principles. What are these ways? Well,
in attempting to decide between rival sets of first
principles, the age and utility of the respective sets
should count for something. If one set has lasted lon-
ger and done harder work than another then this is
something to count in its favour. What Newman is doing
here is suggesting a kind of pragmatic test, akin to
the erstwhile context-invariant tests of predictive
success, fertility, simplicity, as used in the philosophy of science in an attempt to decide a similar
issue.

Let us look at one of Newman´s examples. Consider
a Protestant and a Catholic disputing about the possibility of miracles occurring in our own era. The Protestant has something like this as a first principle:
"What God did once he is not likely to do again, so,
miracles are not likely to occur." The Catholic has as
a first principle "What God did once he is likely to do

again, so, miracles are likely to occur often." The issue between them is not really one of fact. It is a question of first principles. Both take their respective first principles to be true and, as Newman is the first to admit, both have a right to consider their first principles to be true until they are disproved. It is here that Newman makes a curious claim. A Protestant, he tells us, ought to prove his first principle true before he uses it to criticize others. What Newman is primarily interested in disputing here is the right of a person to use his first principles outside their proper sphere. Even so, in insisting that the Protestant prove his first principles, Newman has forgotten that earlier he had stated that first principles are such that they cannot be proved. What is the point of requiring that the Protestant do something which it is not possible to do. There can be no obligation where there is no possibility of fulfilling that obligation.

The Protestant's first principles are, according to Newman, his spontaneous judgement, his instinctive feeling, his common sense. As such there is nothing to be said against them. However, they are also his private opinions, i.e. not universal, not instincts ranging through time and space and, as such, they are defective. Newman clearly vacillates on the matter of proving first principles. First principles, he tells us, are commonly not proved; rather they are assumed. This again is testimony in favour of the existence of distinct classes of first principles. If, as seems to be the case, some first principles are capable of being proven, then this suggests that there are at least two classes of first principles: unprovable first principles, and provable first principles. Newman now goes on to give us a hint as to what a proof of a first principle consists in. The Catholic first principle in the case of miracles above, admits, if not of proof, at least of recommendation because of the antecedent presumption created by the fact of the Incarnation. This is obviously not proof in the sense of a demonstration, i.e. the propositions to be recommended do not follow deductively from other propositions. Such recommended first principles are what we would have expected given our antecedent assumptions, they explain all the data satisfactorily, they link up with previously held beliefs, etc.

Newman, finally, offers these suggestions for adoption in cases of apologetic. When confronted with another's first principles, we are to attempt to get him to determine whether those first principles are universal or merely local, national, or temporary. We can further ask our interlocutor to determine whether his first principles function foundationally, and whether they have ever accomplished anything great. Let us sum up.

1. First principles are propositions.

2. First principles are assumed.

3. First principles have no grounds.

4. First principles cannot be proved.

5. First principles are the means of proving other propositions.

6. First principles are either true or false, i.e. not necessarily true.

7. First principles are held unavoidably.

8. First principles are arrived at inexplicably.

9. First principles are our perspective on life and its activities.

10. First principles constitute our mental life.

11. First principles can in some way be recommended by antecedent assumptions.

12. Some first principles don't come within reach of the facts at all.

13. There are ways of unlearning first principles when they are false.

This set of characteristics is not perfectly consistent. For example, first principles are propositions (1) and yet they also appear to be innate dispositions (9,10). First principles are assumed (2) which suggests that one has some choice as to whether one holds them or not; yet, first principles are also held unavoidably (7) which suggests the contrary. From (3,4) we know that first principles cannot be proved, yet, according to (11) first principles can be recommended by antecedent assumptions and what is this recommendation is not some kind of proof? Finally, Newman as-

serts that there are ways of unlearning first principles when they are false (13) yet how is this to be
squared with (7,8) which assert that first principles
are held unavoidably, are inexplicably arrived at, and
don't come within reach of the facts at all?

The criteria for distinguishing true first principles from false first principles appear to be

1. the universality of their reception

2. their age

3. their utility

4. the universality of the instinct which pro-
    duced them (variant of the first point)

5. their recommendation via antecedent assump-
    tions.

With regard to these points: the first is such
that any first principle which is universally received
is necessarily true. The remaining four points bear no
such necessary relationship to truth.

Prejudices, as contrasted with first principles, are beliefs held against reason having grounds which the holder of the prejudice refuses to examine.[43] The criteria for distinguishing first principles from pre-judices would appear to be:

1. First principles are _prior_ to reason; pre-judices are _against_ reason.

2. If a belief is _a priori_ then it is not a prejudice. Its aprioricity is sufficient to make a belief a _first principle_ though not sufficient to make it a _true_ first principle.

Now the treatment of first principles in the _Grammar_ is not as thematic as it is in _Present Position of Catholics_. The longest sustained account of first principles is to be found in the section on "Presump-tion." ´Presumption´ is defined as ´assent to first principles.´ First principles in turn are character-ised thus:

1. First principles are the propositions with which we start to reason on any given subject-matter.

2. First principles are elementary truths prior to reason.

3. First principles are the recondite sources of all our knowledge.

4. Logic provides no common measure with regard to first principles.

5. First principles are called self-evident because they are evident in no other way.[44]

6. First principles are very numerous.

7. First principles vary from one person to another according to

   1. judgement

   2. power of assent.

8. Only a few first principles are received universally.

If we examine this list carefully we shall become aware of a tension similar to the one we detected in the list of characteristics of first principles as found in Catholics. First principles are truths prior to reasoning (2); contrast this with (6-8) which stress the multiplicity and relativity of first principles. In addition, (2) on this list conflicts with (6) on the Catholics list. There, it will be remembered, Newman was emphatic that first principles were not necessarily true. These considerations indicate that (2) on this list will need to be modified if it is to apply to the whole class of first principles.

Our trust in our powers of reasoning and memory are commonly taken to be first principles, i.e. as expressed in the proposition "Our reason and our memory are to be trusted." In Newman's opinion, this is a philosophical solecism. We can't properly be said to trust our powers. of reasoning and memory (though we can trust particular acts of reason and memory.)[45] So, Newman denies that the proposition expressing trust in our reasoning and memory is a first principle. According to Newman, the proposition "There are things existing external to ourselves" is a first principle and, indeed, one that is universally received. This first principle is founded on an instinct (because brutes possess it in common with man). It is directed towards individual phenomena and it is pre-rational. In contrast with brutes, humans draw from their recurring experience a general proposition, i.e. through an inductive process they arrive at the proposition "There are things existing external to ourselves."[46] We apprehend the reality of individual phenomena by instinct but not the truth of the general proposition. Our instinct apprises us of the reality of individual phenomena. We then inductively conclude from these particular experiences that there is an external world of which these phenomena are particular manifestations. Newman draws a close analogy between sense and conscience in regard to their instinctive power. As on the basis of sense experience, through instinct, we perceive isolated items of physical reality which, via induction, become aspects of a unified external world, so too, on the basis of our experience of conscience through instinct we perceive isolated mandates which, via induction, become aspects of a Sovereign Ruler. Here are some examples of first principles in this area:

1. There is a right and a wrong.

2. There is a true and a false.

3. There is a just and an unjust.

4. There is a beautiful and a deformed.

These are abstractions to which we give notional assent in consequence of particular experiences of the concrete to which we give real assent.[47] The sequence is as follows: we experience approbation and take it to be a manifestation of virtue. We experience pleasure and take it to be a manifestation of beauty. These so-called first principles are really abstractions or conclusions from particular experiences; that is, they are abstractions from facts, not elementary truths prior to reasoning and hence it seems, are not really first principles. (That, presumably, is the force of ´so-called.´) The problem with this is that, if anything is a paradigmatic first principle, "There is an external world" is one. Yet this is abstracted from particular concrete experiences. If a proposition´s being an abstraction from facts disqualifies it from being a first principle, then it disqualifies that which Newman has unreservedly called a first principle, viz. "There is an external world." Yet, if we allow

Newman's 'so-called' first principles to really be first principles then it seems as if first principles cannot simply be elementary truths prior to reasoning. The problem is insoluble until it is realized that here we have just another instance of Newman's conflation of intuition and inference. The abstraction which precedes the establishment of these 'so-called' first principles is not inference: it is intuition. Hence, these are all genuine first principles.

Newman's notion of prejudice in the Grammar differs significantly from that of Catholics. In the Grammar prejudice is distinguished from certitude by being characterized as "assent prior to rational grounds." (Certitude, it will be remembered, followed upon some inferential process or other.) The problem with this characterisation of prejudice is that at least some first principles are assents prior to rational grounds. Are these first principles then prejudices? According to the characterization given they must be. Using the term 'prejudice' in this way, however, evacuates it of all pejorative connotations. It becomes simply a rather odd synonym for first principles. If Newman wished the term to retain its pejorative connotations, he should have retained the characterization he gave of it in Catholics, where prejudice was defined as a belief held tenaciously against reason rather than one simply held prior to reason. In moving from Catholics to the Grammar Newman´s notion of prejudice has become somewhat equivocal. The use of the term ´prejudice´ signifies that Newman wants it to convey a negative message. However, as defined, it is simply coterminous with the class of first principles.

I have suggested that there is a tension in Newman´s characterisation of first principles, the most plausible interpretation of which is that there are at least two distinct kinds of first principle. Items (3,4,5,7,8,12) of Catholics list and items (2,4) of the Grammar list testify to one kind of first principle. Items (11,13) of Catholics list and items (6,7,8 and 9) testify to the existence of the other kind. Let us call the first kind of first principle ´absolute´ and the second ´relative.´[48] On my interpretation then, an absolute first principle is one which

* has no grounds
* cannot be proved

* is the means of proving other propositions

* is held unavoidably

* is an elementary truth prior to reasoning

* shares no common ground in logic with other first principles.

Examples of absolute first principles are:

* There are things external to ourselves.

* There is a right and a wrong.

* There is a true and a false.

* There is a just and an unjust.

* We have a duty to be just, true, and temperate.

Relative first principles, on the other hand,

* can be recommended by antecedent assumptions

* can be unlearned when they are false.

Examples of relative first principles are:

* Man is a social being.

* Man may defend himself.

* There is no evil so great in the whole world as humiliation.

* What God has done once he is likely to do again.

* What God has done once he is not likely to do again.

254

To see if a theoretical underpinning can be provided for this distinction, let us examine the meta-metaphysical theories of R.G. Collingwood.[49]

Collingwood

In Collingwood's case we are going to be dealing with what he calls presuppositions. Presuppositions are those elements in Collingwood which correspond roughly to first principles in Newman. In order to understand what Collingwood means here we have to understand that the theory of presuppositions is situated within a context of a logic of question and answer. According to Collingwood, all statements are responses to some logically prior question. Questions, in turn, can only be asked against the background of some previous supposition, or set of suppositions. This contextual necessity is a logical one, i.e. a certain question can only arise on the basis of some presupposition or other. (There may be, and very likely is, more than one such presupposition. But there must be at least one.) An example Collingwood uses is this: we can ask a man whom we know to be an uxorious husband whether he has stopped beating his wife. But the question "Have you stopped beating your wife" is based on (arises from) the presupposition that he has been in the habit of beating her. Since we know this not to be the case, the question "Have you stopped beating your wife" cannot logically arise. Collingwood terms the ability of a given presupposition to give rise to questions, its ´logical efficacy.´ The logical efficacy of a presupposition does not depend on its being true, merely on its being supposed.[50] This fact might seem somewhat surprising at first but if follows from what Collingwood has said so far. If the logical efficacy of a presupposition is its ability to give rise to questions, then false presuppositions can generate questions just as well as true presuppositions. Unfortunately, Collingwood is not simply allowing for the possibility that presuppositions may be false as well as true; he espouses the much more radical doctrine that absolute presuppositions, as absolute presuppositions, cannot have truth value.

Collingwood distinguishes two types of presupposition; relative presuppositions and absolute presuppositions. An absolute presupposition is defined as "one which stands relatively to all questions to which it is related, as a presupposition, never as an answer."[51] A relative presupposition is defined as "one which stands relatively to one question as its presupposition and relatively to another as its answer."[52]

A relative presupposition is a proposition which, for the purposes of a certain activity, is accepted without question, but which is not, outside the scope of that activity, totally unquestionable. For example, asking and answering questions about the distance from New York to Chicago, or the weight of a bag of apples, presupposes that our measuring apparatuses are accurate, within an acceptable margin of error. But of course, it is not unknown for these measuring apparatuses to be defective and so, from time to time, we need to ask this question: "Is this meter stick/scales/chain accurate?" Collingwood calls this process of asking questions about presuppositions 'verification.'[53] Collingwood's point here is that we can ask questions about these presuppositions without being absurd. It is here that the difference between absolute presuppositions and relative presuppositions is to be found. Relative presuppositions can be verified; absolute presuppositions cannot. Using Collingwood's own example, let us imagine the following series of questions and answers:

* What is the cause of event E?
* The event C.
* Did E have a cause?
* Of course!
* How can you be sure that E had a cause?
* Because everything that happens has a cause.
* How do you know that?

Absolute presuppositions are not verifiable. This is so, not because it is a difficult task to verify them but because it is impossible. To attempt to verify an absolute presupposition is to treat it as if it were a relative presupposition. There is no question which is logically prior to an absolute presupposition; it is logically prior to all questions. The activity of asking the following kind of question about absolute presuppositions is dubbed by Collingwood "pseudo-metaphysics": Is this absolute presupposition true? What evidence do we have for this absolute presupposition? How can we demonstrate this absolute presupposition? What right have we to presuppose this absolute presupposition if we can't demonstrate it? The attempt to ask and answer such questions is, according to Collingwood, sheer nonsense – not truth, not error, just nonsense. True metaphysics is the task of classifying absolute presuppositions into groups, establishing their origins, and determining which group of people have held them.[54]

What do absolute presuppositions do? How do they function? These questions have already been answered. Absolute presuppositions serve to allow a whole series of questions to arise, making it possible to ask and answer them sensibly. Collingwood stresses that the relationship between absolute presuppositions and what they give rise to is not a truth-functional one, where the truth of the absolute presupposition serves as the ground of the truth of the question/answer series. It is, rather, a semantic relationship, where the question/answer series makes sense because of the supposition of the absolute presupposition. Absolute presuppositions then serve to divide questions into two groups; those that do, and those that do not arise. Since what Collingwood terms metaphysics is the historical study of the changing fortunes of sets of absolute presuppositions, it is manifestly obvious that absolute presuppositions must be subject to historical change. Absolute presuppositions vary diachronically and synchronically. They vary synchronically when one has simultaneously existing sets of different absolute presuppositions. They vary diachronically when the same identifiable social group espouses one set of absolute presuppositions at time t and another at time t + 1. For the moment I am going to focus on diachronic diversity. How does this change occur? Although this question is rather an obvious one and (given Collingwood's own definition of metaphysics) evidently permissible, it had not occurred to Collingwood to ask it of himself. It was brought to his attention by a friend. Collingwood's answer comes in a lengthy footnote in the Essay on Metaphysics.[55] First, Collingwood refuses to allow that change is a matter of choice. The argument for this thesis goes as follows:

1. People are not ordinarily aware of their absolute presuppositions.

2. They are not aware of changes in their absolute presuppositions.

3. Therefore, such a change cannot be a matter of choice.

So much for what can't be done. What has Collingwood to say positively?

> The absolute presuppositions of any given society, at any given phase of its history, form a structure which is subject to 'strains'...of greater or lesser intensity, which are 'taken up' in various ways, but never annihilated. If the strains are too great, the structure collapses and is replaced by another, which will be a modification of the old with the destructive strain removed; a modification not consciously devised but created by a process of unconscious thought.[56]

We immediately ask "What are these strains?" and "How are they taken up?" Collingwood refers us to subsequent portions of his book for elucidation.[57] When we refer to these elucidatory passages we find out that one historical phase succeeds another historical phase because the first phase was in a state of unstable equilibrium.[58] This, however, is not an explanation of what is meant by 'strain,' simply a reaffirmation of its existence.

Collingwood tells us elsewhere that at any given time, the current absolute presuppositions of a given system are consupponible only under pressure, kept together by compromise and mutual toleration.[59] The same comment applies to this case as to the former: it is not an explanation, but a reaffirmation. (Pseudo-metaphysics is castigated for its misguided attempt to uncover tensionless sets of absolute presuppositions from which suitable deductions can be made.)

Even with the paucity of examples it is still possible to get the general idea of what Collingwood is up to. A given historical phase is constituted by various sets of absolute presuppositions, not all of which are perfectly compatible with others. The resultant instability acts as a mechanism of change. Pseudo-metaphysicians make two mistakes. First, they suppose it possible to have an historical structure that is perfectly tensionless. Second, as a result of their first mistake, they are at a loss when it comes to explaining how one historical phase develops from another.

Before we go on to consider some critiques of Collingwood´s position it will be interesting to examine one particular absolute presupposition. This absolute presupposition is "God exists." As it is an absolute presupposition it is nonsensical to inquire into the truth status of this ´proposition.´ God´s existence cannot be proved for "God exists" is an absolute presupposition.[60] This interpretation of "God exists" is to be compared with the ´crude´ interpretation given to it by, among others, logical positivists. Logical positivists take "God exists" to mean that there is a being more or less like human beings except enormously magnified and without any human defects.[61] Since it appears to Collingwood that this is a crude misunderstanding of the expression, he is anxious to discover what Christians mean when they say "God exists." He appeals to the Fathers and discovers that, for them, "God exists" is a presupposition and an absolute one to boot. As such it has no truth value and is incapable of being either proved or disproved. As Collingwood is quick to note, the practice of the Church has not always been consonant with such an understanding (e.g. witness the efforts of St. Thomas). Since then "God exists" is an absolute presupposition we can attach the metaphysical rubric to it; then it becomes equivalent to "We presuppose in all our thinking that God exists." A seemingly tense-less proposition has been converted into an historical proposition. (As correlative evidence for this rein-terpretation Collingwood points to the form of the Creeds, all of which begin "I (We) believe...." Accor-ding to Collingwood, Anselm's proof is perfectly in order for, despite appearances to the contrary, its conclusion is not really "God exists" but rather "we stand committed to belief in God."

> An absolute presupposition cannot be undermined by the verdict of ´experience´, because it is the yard-stick by which ´experience´ is judged.[62]

What (if anything) can ´shake´ absolute presuppos-itions? Well, not experience for a start! Absolute presuppositions are not derived from experience; they are brought from the mind to manipulate experience.

> The result of simply presupposing our presupp-ositions, clinging to them by a sheer act of faith, whether or not we know what they are, whether or nor we work out their consequences, is the creation of a religion; and the instit-utions of a religion have this as their object, to consolidate in believers and perpetuate in their posterity the absolute presuppositions which lie at the root of their thought.[63]

The gist of Collingwood's remarks seems to be this; if

p functions as an absolute presupposition then there is no way to rationally support or justify it.

It would have come as no surprise to Collingwood to find his ingenious reinterpretation of "God exists" rejected by the Logical Positivists. He might have been somewhat more surprised at the number of theists who would not be at all happy with his proffered reinterpretation. The reason for their unhappiness is evident. Collingwood's interpretation is good as far as it goes but it doesn't go far enough. It is true that God's existence is (or should be) a presupposition of the thought and action of the theist. It is also true that religious utterances and actions don't always involve an explicit assertion of God's existence. Nevertheless, when we stop to reflect on our thoughts, words, and deeds, we see that we are indeed committed to affirming the existence of God, however difficult it might be to give an adequate characterisation of the God whose existence we are asserting. Collingwood's solution to the problem of 'God-talk' is quixotic. A problem may be easily solved if its existence be denied. Newman's first principles, though functioning in a way that is remarkably similar to Collingwood's presuppositions, nevertheless have a truth value. Newman's problem (or the problem that McCarthy sees Newman as encountering) is to adjudicate between competing sets of absolute first principles. If two absolute first principles are mutually contradictory and universally exhaustive, how are we to decide which, if either, is true? Can Newman offer us any objective criterion to enable us to distinguish true first principles from false first principles? Let us examine McCarthy's account of Newman to see what his answer to this question is.

McCarthy on Newman on First Principles

According to McCarthy, in Catholics, Newman is attempting to distinguish first principles from prejudices and he offers four tests by which to effect this distinction.[64]

1. If the putative first principle has been able to be carried out in practice and has been able to inspire a noteworthy and successful historical movement, then it is a genuine first principle and not a prejudice...

2. If the putative first principle is universally received and has more than local and regional authority, then it is a genuine

first principle and not a prejudice...

3. If the putative first principle is not merely an empirical generalization and does not come "within reach of the facts" at all, then it is a genuine first principle and not a prejudice...

4. If the putative first principle is capable of being shown to be "instinctive" rather than the mere result of "education" and "habit," then it is a genuine first principle and not a prejudice...[65]

Let us examine the passages where these alleged tests are to be found. In the place cited for the first test, Newman says:

Take your First Principles...try to work society by them. You think you can; I say you cannot... My principles...have at least lasted eighteen hundred years; let yours live as many months.[66]

Concerning the second test, this is what Newman actually says:

There are many of these First Principles, as I have called them, which are common to the great mass of mankind, and are therefore true, as having been imprinted on the human mind by its Maker....Others are peculiar to individuals...Other principles are common to extended localities.[67]

Concerning the third test, Newman says:

[T]he obstinate belief that God cannot punish in hell is rather a first principle than a prejudice, because... it can hardly be said to come within reach of the facts at all.[68]

Concerning the fourth test, I can find nothing in the

passage McCarthy cites; (Catholics, p. 301). However, a few pages later we find this:

> [This is] a mere private opinion of his own...not a world-wide opinion, not an instinct ranging through time and space, but an assumption and presumption, which, by education and habit, he had got to think as certain, as much of an axiom, as that two and two make four.[69]

It is clear that in all of these cases with the exception of the third, Newman is distinguishing between true first principles and false first principles and not between first principles and prejudices. In the case of the third test, Newman _is_ distinguishing between first principles and prejudices, the ground of that distinction being whether a proposition is held prior to reason, in which case it is a first principle, or whether it is held against reason, in which case it is a prejudice. Unless false first principles are conflated with prejudices (and Newman does not do this, at least not in Catholics) then McCarthy's criticism of the first, second and fourth tests is going to be vitiated from the start. It is of little value to criticize Newman for failing to do that which he never intended to do.

The only one of the four tests that is intended to discriminate between first principles and prejudices is the third.[70] McCarthy is right in claiming that not all of Newman's examples of first principles are successful if the third test is applied. to them.[71] This being the case, he suggests that there are three options to consider:

1. Discard the third test.

2. Discard the apparent empirical propositions from our list of first principles.

3. Interpret the erstwhile empirical propositions non-empirically.

Unfortunately, none of these options seems to be acceptable. However, there is one option which McCarthy fails to consider, namely, that there are different kinds of first principle: absolute first principles which are prior to reason, and relative first principles which are not. The question could then arise: If relative first principles are not prior to reason, how are they to be distinguished from prejudices? This question forces us to uncover more fully the distinction between first principles and prejudices. Newman has used two terms to distinguish the one from the other: "prior to reason" and "against reason." Now, it seems that pairing these terms would yield four possible types of proposition:

1. Propositions <u>prior</u> to reason but <u>not</u> <u>against</u> reason

2. Propositions <u>prior</u> to reason and <u>against</u> reason

3. Propositions <u>not</u> <u>prior</u> to reason but <u>not</u> <u>against</u> reason

4. Propositions <u>not</u> <u>prior</u> to reason and <u>against</u> reason

Now the first two kinds of proposition are clearly impossible. If a proposition is prior to reason it makes no sense to say of it that it either is, or is not, against reason. These two types of proposition then may be collapsed into one which reads "There are propositions prior to reason." These are absolute first principles. Propositions of the third kind (those neither prior to nor against reason) are relative first principles. Propositions of the fourth kind (those not prior to reason but against reason) are prejudices.[72]

Now we turn to McCarthy's analysis of what he takes to be Newman's list of types of first principles. He focusses his attention on the following passage:

> It is on no probability that we are constantly receiving the informations and dictates of sense and memory, of our intellectual instincts, of the moral sense, and of the logical faculty. It is on no probability that we receive the generalizations of science, and the great outlines of history. These are certain truths; and from them each of us forms his own judgments and directs his own course, according to the probabilities which they suggest to him, as the navigator applies his observations and his charts for the determination of his course. Such is the main view to be taken of the separate provinces of probability and certainty in matters of this world; and so, as regards the world invisible and future, we have a direct and conscious, knowledge of our Maker, His attributes, His Providences, acts, works, and will, from nature and revelation.[73]

In McCarthy's opinion, this passage yields six types of proposition as first principles. We have first principles

* of sense

* of memory

* of intellectual instincts and logical faculty

* of scientific generalizations and historical outlines

* of moral sense

* of God from nature and Revelation.[74]

McCarthy intends to apply his four tests to each category of proposition. However, as we have seen, only the third test is applicable and even that, if I am right, serves only to distinguish absolute first principles from relative first principles. Still, McCarthy has interesting things to say on each of these categories of first principles.

* SENSE

In considering propositions of sense, McCarthy distinguishes two kinds: (1) propositions of the form "this or that object with this or that property exists.", and (2) the proposition "There is an external world." McCarthy allows that propositions of the first kind are first principles, being based on instinct (or what I would call intuition.) Concerning the second kind of proposition, he says:

> In spite of what Newman said, the proposition "There is an external world" cannot be the conclusion of an inductive argument. This is so because the general premiss of such an argument would entail the truth of the conclusion in question.[75]

Leaving aside the fact that Newman does not really mean

by induction what McCarthy thinks he means by induction, this still supports my contention that the proposition "There is an external world" is not the product of an inference but rather an intuition.

* MEMORY

Newman's point here is that memory propositions have a referring character, just as the propositions of sense do. They are instinctive, like sense propositions, and hence genuine first principles.

* INTELLECTUAL INSTINCTS AND THE LOGICAL FACULTY

The logical faculty can be concerned with either analytic propositions, or complex propositions expressing valid derivation. This is about all that can be said by way of comment on this category of propositions. Concerning instinctive beliefs, McCarthy claims that there are two kinds: beliefs that are original and instinctive and beliefs which result from acts of the reason that are themselves instinctive.[76] The beliefs resulting from the acts of inference, however instinctive the acts might be, are not instinctive in the same sense as the original instinctive beliefs.

The word ´instinctive´ seems to be used in two senses:
(1) instinctive = df. original, underived, non-inferential; (2) instinctive = df. resulting from instinctive process, derived, inferential.

The important question is, which of the two senses is applicable to first principles when they are described as being instinctive? Some Newman texts seem to signify the first sense of ´instinctive´, but Newman gives no criterion for telling when a belief is originally instinctive. Other texts seem to signify the second sense of ´instinctive´. It seems to me that McCarthy is correct in detecting an ambiguity in the Newman texts. But it also seems to me that the solution is obvious. There are two kinds of first principle. There are those which are original, underived and non-inferential; these are absolute first principles: and there are those that result from some instinctive inferential process (albeit at the most tacit level); these are relative first principles.[77]

McCarthy makes one final comment to the effect that ´instinct´ (or as I should call it ´intuition´) does not allow us to distinguish true first principles from false first principles. But of course, as should be obvious by now, ´instinct´ was never intended to distinguish true first principles from false first principles, so Newman can hardly be faulted if it fails to do so.

* GENERALIZATIONS OF SCIENCE, ETC.

These are of quite a different character from the propositions in the preceding categories. McCarthy claims that the point Newman is making here is that

> [A]t any given point in time, both historical and scientific inquirers do not simply begin from the beginning but rather build upon the work of their predecessors and frequently take the conclusions of the past as the unchallenged starting points for their own investigations.[78]

All this goes to show, on my interpretation, is that none of the propositions in this category are absolute first principles; they are, one and all, relative first principles.

* MORAL SENSE

Conscience is a cognitive faculty in its own right and it operates instinctively just as sense and memory do. Sensory impressions lead inexorably to material objects, so moral impressions lead inexorably to our apprehension of real moral qualities (and, presumably, to the moral subject in which they are located.) As McCarthy notes "such propositions as ´Truth is praiseworthy´ are as self-evident as any of the propositions with which we express our belief in the existence of the external world"[79] Conscience is an original cognitive faculty and is not dependent on the testimony of the other faculties.

* PROPOSITIONS ABOUT THE INVISIBLE WORLD, ETC. AND REVELATION

McCarthy notes, correctly, that Newman has a somewhat ambivalent attitude towards natural theology. He agrees with P. Flanagan that

[W]hile Newman was an Anglican he seemed to distrust the traditional proofs for God´s existence but...upon his conversion to Roman Catholicism, he valued the intellectual cogency of these arguments more highly while remaining sceptical of their religious value.[80]

Concerning propositions derived from Revelation, McCarthy points out that

One theme that appears with considerable frequency throughout his works is that the morally or religiously sensitive mind will have an "instinctive" attraction for revealed truth and an "instinctive" aversion from religious error.[81]

The upshot of the foregoing chapters is, according to McCarthy, that Newman fails to establish criteria that are both necessary and sufficient to distinguish between epistemically legitimate assumptions and epistemically illegitimate assumptions.[82] McCarthy now proposes his own interpretation of the role of first principles in Newman's thought. In his attempt to establish the necessity for foundational propositions it appears that Newman gave two arguments: the first attempts to show that there must be a stopping place in a justificational regress; and the second attempts to show that these stopping places are incapable of being proved.[83] These two arguments have associated with them two corresponding forms of foundationalism:

1. Regress Foundationalism: Here, first principles are self-evident propositions, known intuitively to be true. They are absolute, self-justifying beginnings for justificatory procedures.

2. Presuppositional Foundationalism: In this case, to avoid scepticism, we make assumptions which are neither deductively nor inductively justified but are still required for the jus-

tification of what we know. These propositions don´t derive their epistemic warrant from any peculiar property which they possess. They derive their warrant from the propositions for which they serve as foundations.

In any given linguistic system there will be certain propositions that are unconditionally assertable within those systems. McCarthy employs the following definitions:

1. Linguistic System (L) = df. a body of propositions governed by rules that express the necessary and permissible relations among the propositions which constitute the system.

2. P is unconditionally assertible in L = df. the truth of p is not contingent upon the truth of any other proposition in L.

These propositions have this unconditionally assertible character not because of any intrinsic property but because of the role they play within the system, i.e. they are neither epistemically nor ontologically primary, simply functionally primary.[84]

There are many linguistic systems. Many of these linguistic systems have propositions in common: observation propositions, for example, but other kinds as well. For example, the linguistic systems ´common-sense´ and ´science´ share a large body of propositions in common as do the linguistic systems ´common-sense´ and ´ethics.´

How do unconditionally assertible propositions receive their position in a linguistic system? They do so by being presupposed by all the other propositions in the system. McCarthy proposes this semantic definition of ´presuppose´:

> * P presupposes q = df. not-q implies that p can be neither true nor false.[85]

Many common-sense statements presuppose that there are states of affairs which are extra-mental. Moral injunctions presuppose the existence of moral obligations. The unconditionally assertible status of these propositions is system dependent, i.e. if the system goes, they also go (provided that no other system presupposes them.) We have instances of whole systems disappearing, and with them their unconditionally assertible propositions, for example, witchcraft.[86]

How does all this apply to Newman? Well, according to McCarthy, Newman gave us three definitions of certitude.[87] The strong definition of certitude (definition 2) applies only to system-relative propositions. So, within a system a proposition may be certain (or we may have certitude about it) in the sense of the second definition. However, it is an obvious fact that there are competing linguistic systems. The replacement or abandonment of linguistic systems is not always an arbitrary matter. Operative in choices between competing linguistic systems are such system-invariant criteria as, simplicity, theoretical elegance, fidelity to data, etc.[88] These criteria are pragmatic and their application can yield only the weak sense of certitude, certitude 1.

McCarthy wants to redefine Newman's terms. Let 'certainty' = df. 'the property of an intra-systemic foundational proposition.' So, propositions can only be certain within systems. Sub specie aeternitatis we can only have 'certitude' concerning x (i.e. the weak sense of certitude) because given the lack of clear decision-procedures for choosing the system of which x is a part, we really have no ultimately secure justification for asserting x. To put it another way, we can say that, given system S, with component proposition p, we are entitled to be certain of p. But since system S as a whole is itself not absolutely certain we really have only ´certitude´ concerning p when it is considered in abstraction from the system of which it is the foundation.[89]

McCarthy makes a few points about this material. First, the warrants for assertions differ in explicitness from one system to another (i.e. the foundational propositions are more readily apparent in some systems than in others.) In choosing between systems, since there are a variety of criteria, it may happen that some criteria will apply to system A and others to system B. There is no clear-cut way to justify our adoption of either system A or system B but this is not to say that such choices are irrational. The people who choose do give reasons for their choice and they also believe that to doubt the propriety of their choice is irrational. As McCarthy notes this is only weak certitude.

It does not seem apparent to me that the two types of foundationalism which McCarthy distinguishes are ultimately distinct. For example, Collingwood uses the regress argument to establish the need for presuppositions. Newman too uses the regress argument. It seems that McCarthy is confusing the process of becoming aware of our first principles with the process of recognizing our first principles as first principles.[90] It seems to me that McCarthy is confusing what might be called the first and third person perspectives. What I have a right to be certain of cannot be limited by what I can persuade others to be certain of. Ultimately I am the judge of what I an entitled to be certain of. One of the factors (but only one) which will go into my decision will be the judgement of others as to what is rational and acceptable. But were all the world against me, it is still possible that I should be certain of my certainties and be justified in my certainty.

Finally, McCarthy's account of first principles as presuppositions with no perceived character of basicality makes the selection of such first principles somewhat of a mystery. Why are first principles chosen to be (or recognized as being) first principles unless it be that they possess some manifest characteristic which fits them for that role?

McCarthy's distinction between intra-systemic pro-position and inter -systemic propositions brings up the question of rational choice between competing sets of first principles. To this question we now turn. Before I discuss Newman's position on this issue I would like to review some articles that deal with the same topic and which will be useful in helping us to distinguish the relevant factors.

Whittier and others on Basic Assumptions

The first article, by D.H.Whittier, is concerned with the reasons we have for adopting or abandoning what he calls 'basic assumptions' or presuppositions.[91] His thesis is that in a dispute between holders of different basic assumptions the 'arguments,' with their attendant examples and analogies, are illuminating only if one is already committed to the given basic assumption or set of assumptions. What is offered by the protagonists is not so much an argument as an articulation of how they are viewing the world. In a

dispute based on different basic assumptions we can

expect to find the articulation of incompatible posit-

ions rather than arguments based on common grounds.

The basic problem is, how do we decide between opposing

presuppositions?

Whittier makes use of W.B.Gallie's notion of an

'essentially contested concept.' An essentially con-

tested concept is such that its use is not governed by

language rules, or, in its case, the language rules are

called into question. As an example of an essentially

contested concept Whittier instances 'causation' as

used by Hume and Whitehead respectively.

Hume argued that we do not perceive (have a
sense impression of) the connection between a
cause and its effect. Whitehead replied that
Hume's statement is false. E.g., between a
bright flash of light as a cause and blinking as
effect we experience the connection (the feeling
of strain is the impression of the cause making
its effect). Stace has replied to Whitehead for
Hume by pointing out that even if this is so, we
do not perceive the connection between the flash
and the strain. And even if someone were able
to point to an impression of something lying
between the flash-impression and the
strain-impression, we could still ask whether
between those two impressions we find the impression of a 'connection'. The threat of the
infinite regress looms here. Now non-Humean
philosophers would conclude from all this that
Hume and Stace have got hold of a gimmick -- a
question that in principle can never be silenced. On this ground non-Humeans would reject

Hume's reasoning as illegitimate. To ask a question that in principle cannot be silenced' is to ask an unfair or trick question. But this very fact that non-Humeans appeal to as the exposure of the trick is the very fact that Humeans appeal to as proof-positive that they are right and have found a firm, undeniable truth. So once again we have something that is 'essentially contested' -- whether a question that in principle can never be silenced is to be considered a truth of reason or a mischievous linguistic habit.[92]

Reasons in philosophical argument do not lead to verdicts; rather, verdicts are selected on intuitive grounds and guide. the selection of reasons to be used in support of the verdicts. "All philosophical thought involves the making of basic assumptions." These basic assumptions have the status of being essentially contested for there is no established decision procedure for choosing among them. Whittier's thesis is as follows

It is not possible to argue for or against assumptions. True; in actual practice, reasons are given with the intention of supporting various basic presuppositions. But such reasons can be judged 'good' reasons only from within the perspective of the basic presupposition for which the reason is being given....All arguing for presuppositions is circular and where there is circularity, there is no genuine argument at all.[93]

However, according to Whittier, though we cannot argue for our basic assumptions we can 'contend' concerning them. Contending is an attempt to get our opponent to shift his frame of reference. There is basically only one way of contending and that is by means of an ad hominem argument. We try to show that one of our opponent´s basic assumptions implies p, where p is a proposition our opponent overlooked and is also one he doesn´t want to commit himself to.94 If we succeed in our endeavour, we have caught our opponent, not in a formal inconsistency, but in a conflict of allegiances.

> [A]ll fundamental philosophical disputation is and must be ad hominem. (An ad hominem argument is one that rubs an opponent´s nose in the incompatibility of his allegiances.) No pressure can be exerted against an opponent that does not derive from the inconsistencies of his explicit and implicit commitments. All one can do is contend with him over one of his presuppositions in the hope that he will lose his desire to assert it.95

Basic assumptions are abandoned if an ad hominem argument either exposes a conflict of allegiances or the concepts in the basic assumption become opaque or unintelligible. Basic assumptions are never refuted; they are outgrown or become obsolete.

Peter Schouls approaches the same problem from a slightly different angle.96 He is concerned with the problem of philosophical communication which he defines

as "philosophical discussion or argumentation based on
mutual understanding by those engaged in the discussion
of one another's philosophical position."[97] Schouls
makes use of two concepts. Two philosophical positions
are mutually exclusive if each involves elements basic
to it which are not shared by the other. Two philosophical positions are isolated if, in addition to
being exclusive, there is no possibility of philosophical interaction between them. Exclusive positions are
not necessary isolated; isolated positions are necessarily exclusive. By way of an example of interactive
philosophical argumentation Schouls instances a dispute
between a Platonist and a Kantian.

1. Kantian: The understanding is the law-giver
   of nature.

2. Platonist: This is a presupposition of the
   Kantian system.

3. Kantian: This supposition is proved apodic-
   tically via complex argumentation.

4. Platonist:This appears to be so only because
   it is presuppositional in those arguments.
   Kant's arguments don't establish anything.

They merely make fully explicit the nature of certain presuppositions and show the consequences of their adoption.

5. Kantian: I deny the Platonist's charge and claim there are reasons available for the suppositi on, viz, experience or nature.

6. Platonist: this experience or nature is experience or nature as interpreted in terms of the Kantian position.

And so on.

The nature of philosophical argumentation is determined to a large extent by the presence of presupposition in the positions of those engaged in the discussion, whether this presence is recognized or not.[98] The acceptance of certain concepts despite our inability to argue for our against them means that we commit ourselve to these propositions. A philosophical position arises from a way of thinking about the world. This way of thinking introduces the presuppositions and that on which thought is focussed provides the content. The particular positions or system that results is structured by, but not deductively derivable from, the presuppositions. According to Schouls, although the Kantian and the Platonist both have totally different definitions of ´law´, they are still both interested in the same thing. He considers the obvious objection

> If it is said that because of their different definitions of "law" they are not really interested in the same thing, it can be pointed out that this criticism does not hold because both are interested in what makes the world "dependable," or in what is the "structure" of reality. Although, because of different definitions of "law" their account of this "dependability" or "structure" differs, it is undeniable that both attempt an account of the same thing.[99]

Appeal to ´experience´ or ´fact´ in philosophy is irrelevant because specific presuppositions determine just what is experience and just what is a fact. Facts function in argument only as interpreted. Can we appeal to logic? Yes, but logic doesn´t give reasons for adopting or abandoning presuppositions.[100] If I abandon one set of presuppositions I can only be _persuaded_ to accept another. It (the second set) cannot be _proved_ to me by either factual evidence or by logical demonstration. We cannot argue: we can only proclaim.

> [A] philosophical argument...never establishes anything conclusively...There have never been any absolutely cogent reasons for parting with the law of excluded middle, accepting Darwinism, giving up the Ptolemaic system or renouncing the principle of causality...conflicts of this type

cannot be resolved...either by adducing factual evidence or by logical demonstration...a "welt-anschauung" like that of Kant or...even a new approach like that of Wittgenstein is never 'arrived at,' in particular it is not deduced, and once found it can neither be proved nor refuted by strictly logical reasoning.[101]

What Whittier calls contending, Schouls prefers to call arguing. However, the advocacy or recommendation of your position to the apostate is neither contending nor arguing; it is proclamation. In the case of adherents to rival sets of presuppositions, neither one can understand why the other commits himself to those presuppositions. There is no real understanding of one another's philosophical position as a whole, therefore, there is no full philosophical communication either. Persuasion is not the result of philosophical argumentation.

Discussion between partisans of the same philosophical standpoint, Schouls calls "dialogical-philosophical discussion." It is dialogue because it is a collaborative investigation of the same problem by two philosophers who share a common set of presuppositions. Philosophic argumentation, as interaction between adherents of mutually exclusive philosophic positions, is really concerned only with the more explicit articulation of these positions.

J.King-Farlow replies to Schouls as follows.[102] If Schouls´s thesis were that two good philosophers can understand each other throughly and yet disagree, so that they may need methods other than a priori deductive or a posteriori inductive arguments to break the deadlock, then King-Farlow would not be very distressed. But Schouls´s thesis seems to be concerned with the impossibility of full understanding or communication where presuppositions are different and the impossibility of rationally breaking such deadlocks when rival presuppositions are at stake. King-Farlow suspects Schouls of stretching the meaning of the term ´presupposition´ to include any rule or view built in to a commonly shared and understood language. King-Farlow proposes the following as requirements for the possibility of any rational argument whatsoever:

1. Some views in philosophy are plainly wiser than others.

2. We have good reason to believe (1) to be true.

3. We have good reason to reject the negation of (1), or the assertion of (2) as unintelligible.

4. (1)-(3) provide a base for philosophical reunion.

5. If S systematically rejects (1)-(3), we have reason to rejects S's claim to be a philosopher with whom it is worth arguing.

6. If S tries to argue with us about what is the case in a rational manner while rejecting (1)-(3), then his claims are likely to be in a philosophically unacceptable conflict with with themselves, either as a matter of logic or semantics, or as a matter of rational practices in communication.

7. There is good reason to believe that we are commited to the existence of a Natural Light of Human Reason capable, in a limited way, of discriminating what is more likely to be true, good, wise, etc., from what is not likely to be so.

8. To argue seriously with anyone presupposes
    one's commitment to (6). (6) is not an arbit-
    rary Schoulsian presupposition but a universal
    and indispensable binding rule.

The inability to vindicate oneself to others does
not prove that presuppositions make lack of understanding and progress inevitable. For example, we do
not have to swallow the Schoulsian Kantian, or the
Schoulsian Platonist whole. We can find reasons for
accepting some parts of the Kantian or Platonist position and rejecting other parts. While it is true that
I may fail to accept a philosophical position because I
fail to understand it, it is also eminently possible
that I may reject it because I understand it only too
well![103] According to King-Farlow (and I think he is
right in this) Schouls underestimates the value of
logic. To allow that an unforseen or unwanted implication might undermine a presupposition is to allow that
logic has a role to play. Finally, systems based on
presuppositions can be unsatisfactory not only if they
imply false propositions but also if they fail to imply
the truth of propositions that we need to accept in
order to account for various features of human exis-

tence.

Gary Kodish attacks Schouls from yet another angle.[104] Schouls has defined a presupposition as a proposition related in an extra-logical way to the proposition which presupposed it. According to Kodish, this extra-logical relation is either semantic, or pragmatic. Kodish expresses the relation as follows. A proposition (a) is a presupposition of another proposition (b) if, in order to understand (b), one must first understand (a). If there is to be any intelligibility, this account of the relationship between propositions demands an end point, i.e. a proposition which presupposes no other. Kodish calls this a basic presupposition. He sketches Schouls's argument as follows:

1. Commitment to a philosophical school involves commitment to a set of basic presuppositions belonging to that school.

2. A necessary condition of philosophic communication is a mutual understanding of two (or more) distinct and contradictory sets of basic presuppositions.

3. To understand a basic presupposition is ipso facto, to be commited to it.

4. No one can be rationally commited to two distinct sets of basic presuppositions.

5. Therefore, the necessary condition (2) is impossible.

6. Therefore, scholastic intercommunication is impossible, and

7. It is impossible for a person to understand more than one distinct school of philosophy.

The third of these points is false. Is Schouls commited to it? Yes, according to Kodish. A philosopher understands the basic presuppositions to which he is commited. Since no reason for holding a basic presupposition can be given to the uncommited, then that basic presupposition must remain unintelligible to them. So, commitment is co-extensive with intelligibility.[105]

Whittier and Schouls have shown that, in regard to competing systems of basic presuppositions, all we can have recourse to is internal or _ad_ _hominem_ criticism.

More positively, we can resort to ˊproclamation.ˊ King-Farlow is right in his criticism of Schouls. Schouls does not very clearly distinguish the two senses of ˊunderstandingˊ necessary to make his position tenable: understanding the internal consistency of your opponentˊs postion; and understanding the point of your opponentˊs position (which is equivalent to accepting it.)

Newman

Newman at times makes very strong claims. First principles are essentially at variance with one another, so that those who espouse them will differ from each other at the deepest level. Is this a matter of fact or a matter of principle? There are conflicting texts in Newman. Sometimes he seems to be taking a very hard line, i.e. no possibility of intelligible communication; at other times he seems to allow for the possibility, though with great difficulty. Newmanˊs practice was similarly ambiguous. He corresponded for 30 years with William Froude (whose first principles were avowedly incompatible with his own) but

refused to join the Metaphysical Club on the grounds
that he did not share the first principles of its mem-
bers. Here are some of the texts which support the
´hard´ line. The first comes from the papers of 1860
on "Evidence for Revelation."[106]

> [T]he obvious point to be considered is, <u>can</u> a
> science be of a private personal character, and
> must it not be intelligible to all the world?
> Since reason in religion, is a reasoning of a
> <u>religious</u> mind, it is plain that its fundamental
> axioms will not be intelligible except to relig-
> ious men...to the rest it will be like words
> without meaning. Can this be called a <u>science</u>?
> Aristotle says an <u>episteme</u> [Scientific know-
> ledge] is a necessary deduction from principles;
> and these principles are natural truths, and
> their habit a natural habit. Yet, in like man-
> ner, <u>nous</u> may be <u>supernatural</u> -- and then this
> science is not level to the comprehension of any
> who has not the <u>supernatural</u> habit.

> Antecedent questions

> 1. a proof <u>open</u> <u>to</u> <u>all</u> antecedently likely

> 2. on science, not necessarily being open <u>to</u>
>   <u>all</u> <u>mankind</u>, e.g. if they have not <u>eyes</u>.

The next passage is to be found in "Revelation in
its Relation to Faith."[107]

> [Reasoning] depends for success upon the
> assumption of prior acts similar to that which
> it has itself involved, and therefore is rel-
> iable only conditionally....In the province of
> religion, if it be under the happy guidance of
> the moral sense, and with teachings which are
> not only assumptions in form but certainties in
> fact, it will arrive at indisputable truth...
> But [if it be used by those] who are under the

delusion that their arbitrary assumptions are self-evident axioms, then reasoning will start from false premisses, and the mind will be in a state of melancholy disorder....<u>Half</u> <u>the</u> <u>contro-versies</u> <u>in</u> <u>the</u> <u>world,</u> <u>could</u> <u>they</u> <u>be</u> <u>brought</u> <u>to</u> <u>a</u> <u>plain</u> <u>issue,</u> <u>would</u> <u>be</u> <u>brought</u> <u>to</u> <u>a</u> <u>prompt</u> <u>term-ination.</u> <u>Parties</u> <u>engaged</u> <u>in</u> <u>them</u> <u>would</u> <u>then</u> <u>perceive</u>...<u>that</u> <u>in</u> substance...<u>their</u> <u>difference</u> <u>was</u> <u>of</u> <u>first</u> <u>principles</u>....<u>When</u> <u>men</u> <u>understand</u> <u>what</u> <u>each</u> <u>other</u> <u>means,</u> <u>they</u> <u>see</u> <u>for</u> <u>the</u> <u>most</u> <u>part</u> <u>that</u> <u>controversy</u> <u>is</u> <u>either</u> <u>superfluous</u> <u>or</u> <u>hopeless.</u> (Emphasis added.)

Another passage that supports the ´hard´ line is:

It is not wonderful then, that, while I can prove Christianity divine to my own satis-faction, I shall not be able to force it upon any one else. Multitudes indeed I ought to suc-ceed in persuading of its truth without any force at all, because they and I start from the same principles, and what is a proof to me is a proof to them; but if any one starts from any other principles but ours, I have not the power to change his principles, or the conclusion which he draws from them, any more than I can make a crooked man straight.[108]

Passages which seem to support a softer line in-clude those (already cited) where Newman asserts that the illative sense ´follows out´ ´defends´ ´resists´ the elementary contrarieties of opinion.[109] The mind detects these principles "in their obscure recesses." It "illustrates them, establishes them, eliminates them, resolves them into simpler ideas."[110] However, the ´softness´ of these texts is more apparent than real. Here, the illative sense is operating in its

capacity of noetic faculty, not in its capacity of
architectonic faculty of reasoning. In the second of
these passages the illative sense is not even mentioned
by name. Instead, the active element here is the mind,
or <u>nous</u>. Ward reveals that, in a conversation he had
with him, Newman allowed that first principles could be
indirectly proven.[111] This, however, is nothing more
than Newman has already conceded in his major works.
There he had allowed that some first principles could
be recommended by means of antecedent assumptions. I
accounted for this seeming discrepancy by postulating
the existence of two kinds of first principle. It
seems than as if Newman would agree with Whittier and
Schouls provided that a clear distinction was made between two kinds of understanding or intelligibility:
the first kind being concerned with apprehending the
articulation of an opponent's position; the second
with grasping the point of that system and accepting
it. Is discourse possible between holders of different
first principles? Newman seems to suggest...no! At
least not at the deepest level. Is it then never possible to succeed in changing my own or another's first
principles? It is possible, but not probable. The
possibility rests on a growing together that is not

wholly captured by any simple intellectual agreement. First principles are personal. Is dialogue a waste of time? No. Newman says it uncovers the depth and extent of the differences between men. Consider Abel and Bundy. If Abel wants to convert Bundy to Abel's system then, necessarily, if their first principles differ, he must begin on Bundy's terms. i.e. he must show that Bundy's first principles are in some way deficient. How is he going to do this? By internal criticism, i.e. by showing Bundy's principles to be internally inconsistent, or by showing an inconsistency between his beliefs and his actions. How well can this be done? Well enough within the limitations of language. But as first principles are sometimes expressible in language only with difficulty so the arguments directed towards changing another's first principles, insofar as they are couched in particular linguistic modes, may miss the mark.

Newman was torn between two possibilities. On the one hand, he had no wish to concede that our first principles were the product of an arbitrary choice. So, in some passages, he suggests that the failure of others to grasp and accept our first principles must be due to some moral defect on their part. On the other hand, given his insistence on the personal element in the apprehension of first principles, he seems to suggest that it is possible for two men of good will to be earnest seekers after truth and nevertheless hold to conflicting sets of first principles. His long correspondence with William Froude, a one-time student who later drifted farther and farther from theism convinced Newman that the latter of these two options was correct.[112] Froude was a man of impeccable morals. No fault could be found with his private life. He was also an eminent scientist. His long correspondence with Newman on the matter of their fundamental differences, and his willingness to be convinced, if proof should be forthcoming, of the truth of Newman's position, indicated to Newman that he could not reasonably be convicted of moral or intellectual turpitude. Newman was forced to generalize this conclusion and so allow for the possibility (even though in particular cases it might be extremely improbable) of a basic divergence in the matter of first principles which would be both rationally and morally acceptable.

The choice of first principles is neither a matter of logical compulsion nor a matter of an arbitrary act of the will. Our choice of first principles (which may be, and often is, tacit) is a product of two factors; our moral and intellectual ´complexions,´ and our particular circumstances and experiences. A component of the second factor are what we can call ´objective´ facts; e.g., rules of evidence, shared customs, beliefs, methods of interpretation, norms of rationality, etc. These enter into our beliefs, not as coercive brute facts, but as mediated through our already existent noetic structure. No set of logically necessary and sufficient conditions can then be provided which will eliminate personal responsibilty for our beliefs. On Newman´s view, it appears that our moral and intellectual responsibility for our beliefs and their truth and falsity are independent. The four limiting possibilities of the relationship of moral and intellectual responsibility to truth are as follows:

1. We can be morally and intellectually responsible and have all true beliefs.

2. We can be morally and intellectually responsible and have all false beliefs.

3. We can be morally and intellectually irrespon-
sible and have all true beliefs.

4. We can be morally and intellectually irrespon-
sible and have all false beliefs.

It must be emphasised that none of these possibilities
is probable. They are mere possibilities, no one of
which is more likely to be instantiated than the other.

Summary Conclusion

The chapter began with a glance at some central
Aristotelian notions (Arche, Epagoge, and Nous), in the
hope that they might help shed some light on Newman's
notion of first principles. Then the notions of Prudentia, Noetic Faculty and Illative Sense were discussed. The faculties of Prudentia and Illative Sense
were shown to possess two separate functions which were
later separated and called the Noetic Faculty and Reasoning Faculty. These faculties correspond respectively to intuition and inference. In brief, the con-

flation of inference and intuition that was first located in the notion of natural inference is shown to
permeate also the notions of Illative Sense and Prudentia. The consequences of this conflation for first
principles is that Newman vacillated on the question of
their status in regard to proof. Sometimes it seemed
that first principles could not be proved; at other
times, it seemed as if they could. This difficulty was
explained by postulating two kinds of first principle:
absolute first principles and relative first principles. Finally, the question of discriminating between
competing sets of first principles was considered. It
was shown that, although Newman does not provide us
with a set of necessary and sufficient conditions, he
nevertheless provides some pragmatic ´marks´ which can
enable us to be somewhat less than arbitrary in our
choice of first principles. Ultimately, however, it
was concluded that Newman had to allow for the possibility of equi-rational irreconcilable first principles.
This follows from the nature of first principles and
the nature of the human person.

Notes

¹Posterior Analytics, Book I, Chapter 2, 72a6.

²"Our own doctrine is that not all knowledge is demonstrative: on the contrary, knowledge of immediate premisses is independent of demonstration. The necessity for this is obvious; for since we must know the prior premisses from which the demonstration is drawn, and since the regress must end in immediate truths, these truths must be indemonstrable." Posterior Analytics, Book I, chapter 3, 72b18-23.

³Posterior Analytics, 72b25-73a20.

⁴Posterior Analytics, 99b20-99b33.

⁵Posterior Analytics, 99b33-100a9.

⁶Posterior Analytics, Book II, chapter 19, 100b3-100b5.

⁷Posterior Analytics, Book II, chapter 19, 100b10-100b13.

⁸"Papers on Revelation in Relation to Faith," in Achaval and Holmes, pp. 152-153; 140-157.

⁹Achaval and Holmes, p. 153.

¹⁰Achaval and Holmes, p. 153.

¹¹Newman is well aware that talk of 'faculties' is merely a shorthand way of speaking of the mind and its acts. Such a manner of speaking is not intended to destroy the real unity of the mind.
Of course, for convenience, we speak of the mind as possessing faculties instead of saying that it acts in a certain way and on a definite subject-matter; but we must not turn a figure of speech into a fact.

Achaval and Holmes, p. 155.

¹²"Papers of 1853 on the Certainty of Faith," in Achaval and Holmes, pp. 3-38.

[13]See chapter one for details.

[14]cf. Achaval and Holmes, p. 163; also the Illative Sense in the Grammar, especially the passage (p. 290) where Newman claims that the illative sense discovers and defends ´elementary contrarieties of opinion´ i.e. first principles.

[15]We shall see below when we come to discuss rational choice among first principles that Newman was tempted by two options. On the one hand he had no desire to allow that our first principles were the product of an arbitrary choice. So, in some passages, he suggested that the failure of others to grasp and to accept our first principles must be due to some moral defect on their part. On the other hand, given his insistence on the personal element in the apprehension of first principles, he seemed to suggest that it is possible for two men of good will to seek the truth in earnest and nevertheless hold to conflicting sets of first principles. I shall argue that, because of his experience with William Froude, Newman eventually was forced to abandon the former option and accept the latter.

[16]Grammar, p. 270.

[17]Grammar, p. 271.

[18]Grammar, pp. 272-273.

[19]Grammar, p. 275.

[20]Here again Newman conflates intuition and assent. The illative sense, as the faculty of reasoning, can function legitimately only in the middle and end of inquiry. Since, by definition, the basic premisses of reasoning cannot be established by reasoning, the illative sense cannot function in the beginning of inquiry.

[21]Grammar, p. 282. My italics.

[22]Grammar, p. 290.

[23]Grammar, p. 288.

[24]All the language here suggests intuition rather than inference: "aspects of viewing," "detection," etc.

[25]Grammar, p. 294.

[26]Lecture VII, "Prejudice the Ground of the Protestant View."

[27]Newman is quite explicit here. First principles are groundless; there are no facts on which they are based. We will have to see later how this can be squared with other things Newman says. Note also Newman's stress on the fact that first principles are highly personal; this is what he means by saying they are "part of himself."

[28]A prejudice is something held tenaciously against reason; a prejudgement is something that rests on argumentative grounds. (cf. the Grammar where prejudice is defined as something held prior, but not necessarily against, rational grounds. I will comment on the problems this change of definition causes when I come to deal with prejudice in the Grammar. The distinction between first principles and prejudices is maintained here, though, in the Grammar it collapses. Unfortunately, McCarthy wants to ignore the differences between the two cases. Because Newman chooses to ignore this distiction in the the Grammar, or to express it in another fashion, doesn't warrant concluding that he doesn't make it in Catholics either.

[29]Catholics, p. 279. How are we to unlearn them? Not by examining their grounds, for, ex hypothesi, they have no grounds! Also, given that we can't help holding them, how are we to unlearn them? Newman here hints at the possibility that the previous strong statements concerning groundlessness will have to be taken with a grain of salt.

[30]Catholics, p. 279.

[31]This conclusion is dubious as stated. It is alright if it means that, in a particular discussion, questioning the first principles grounding that discussion will inevitably lead to another topic. So, for example, discussion of topic A operates on the basis of agreed first principles Q. If Q are called into question then we have switched to topic B and this can only take place under another set of first principles, R. This understanding of first principles would force us to view first principles as not all being on the one level, but rather as being arranged in a hierarchical fashion. From a perusal of Newman's examples, it seems clear that first principles are not a homogenous group. Some first principles, such as "There is an external world" seem to be clearly more basic than "A man may defend himself."

[32]As we shall see, this applies properly only to absolute first principles or to all first principles as they are taken to be absolute in the context in which they function as first principles.

[33]Catholics, pp. 283-284.

[34]It is interesting to note in passing that Newman claims that men do not commonly know their first principles because of their dominance and pervasiveness. In this he is at one with Collingwood.

[35]Catholics, p. 285.

[36]Catholics, p. 287.

[37]Of course, the crucial premise here is the second. It is hardly universally received!

[38]Note, in regard to those first principles which are not universal Newman is speaking about authority and not necessarily about truth. It would not follow from the above that that which is particular is necessarily false. From the fact (if it be a fact) that all that is universal is true it does not follow that all that is true is universal. There are strong hints here that the class of first principles is not perfectly homogenous. There seem to be at least two distinct classes of first principles: (1) those which are universal and absolute, and (2) those which are either local or particular, and relative. I shall have more to say of this later.

[39]Catholics, p. 290. ´Assuming´ is an odd word to use if indeed our first principles are such that we cannot help holding them. This is another indication that Newman´s view may be somewhat less obvious that it first appears. Talk of assuming first principles immediately suggests the possibility of not assuming them, or of ceasing to assume them at some given stage. Newman has said that there are ways of unlearning first principles: he has not yet told us what these ways might be.

[40]Newman compares the judging of A´s activities by B´s principles as "valuing English goods by French measures" or "paying debts in paper which were contracted in gold."

[41]Catholics, p. 292.

[42]This may be the place to point out the relativising tendencies of this particular line of thought. What is sauce for the goose is sauce for the gander, and if Catholic practices are not to be criticized on non-Catholic principles, then so too non-Catholic practices are not to be criticized on Catholic principles unless Catholic principles are patently universal and absolute. It is one thing to say "your principles may not operate here for this is our territory, not yours" and another to say "your principles may not operate here, not just because this is our territory, but because they are objectively wrong." Of course we could collapse the two categories, i.e. since your principles are not our principles they are *ipso* *facto* wrong, but this avenue is not open to Newman (even if he wanted to take it) because, as he says, my principles are false if yours are true, not simply because your principles are yours.

[43]See the account below of prejudice in the Grammar.

[44]Grammar, p. 216.

[45]Talk of trusting our reasoning and our memory is akin to wishing that we had had a choice over whether we were created or not, or wondering what we would have been like if born of other parents. Cf. "Proof of Theism," Notebooks, pp. 31-72.

[46]The similarity of this account to that of Aristotle should be obvious. Now, note well that the cited proposition is a first principle yet it is generated by means of induction. It follows then that either this induction (abstraction) is an inferential process and first principles are not prior to proof, despite Newman's assertions, or first principles are prior to proof, in which case induction (abstraction) is not an inferential process. I have argued that the latter half of this disjunction holds.

[47]See Plantinga on "God Exists" as a basic belief, especially the last section of his paper (p. 83) where he admits that "God exists" is not really a basic belief but rather a derivative belief based on such authentic basic beliefs as "God forgives me" etc.

[48]It will turn out that absolute first principles are the product of intuition and relative first principles are the product of inference.

[49]R.G.Collingwood, An Essay on Metaphysics, (Oxford, 1940). See also, S. Toulmin, Human Understanding, (Oxford, 1972), Part I, pp. 52-84; S.Toulmin, "Conceptual Change and the Problem of Relativity,"; M.Krausz, "The Logic of Absolute Presuppositions." (Both these essays are to be found in M.Krausz, ed., Critical Essays on the Philosophy of R.G.Collingwood, (Oxford, 1972.)

[50]Collingwood, p. 28.

[51]Collingwood, p. 31.

[52]Collingwood, p. 29.

[53]Collingwood, p. 30.

[54]This series of question is addressed to a medical man, whose profession, according to Collingwood, is one of the few that still makes the absolute presupposition that "all events have causes."

[55]Collingwood, p. 47. Even given that absolute presuppositions cannot be justified ("verified´) does it follow that they are devoid of truth value? Would it not be possible for a given absolute presupposition to be unjustifiable (´unverifiable´) but still either true of false? The notions of justification and truth are surely independent? This is not so for Collingwood. For a given presupposition to be either true or false is for it to be related as a proposition to some other presupposition. This means, of course, that it is verifiable.

[56]Collingwood, p. 48.

[57]2 follows from 1 if the qualifier ‘ordinarily’ is inserted. But once this is inserted then the contrary argument is cogent:
* People are sometimes aware of their absolute presuppositions.
* They are sometimes aware of changes in their absolute presuppositions.
* Therefore, changing one’s absolute presuppositions can sometimes be a matter of choice.

[58]Collingwood, p. 48, footnote.

[59]Collingwood’s point about strains is basically this; we never have a nice, homogenous set of dominant absolute presuppositions, there is always some incompatibility between them. However, there still remains the problem of justifying one’s choice of absolute presupposition.

[60]Collingwood, p. 74.

[61]Collingwood, p. 76.

[62]Collingwood, p. 132.

[63]Collingwood, p. 185.

[64]Collingwood, pp. 193-194.

[65]Collingwood, p. 197.

[66]McCarthy, pp. 69-77. Throughout this entire section, McCarthy equates false and/or unjustifiable first principles with prejudices. This is an inaccurate assessment of what Newman is saying. In Catholics, false first principles are not the same as prejudices. In fact, by definition, no first principle can be a prejudice. First principles are rational whether false or true; prejudices are anti-rational. (See pp. 173;179;190-191 above.)

[67]McCarthy, pp. 71-72.

[68]Catholics, p. 295.

[69]Catholics, p. 287.

[70]Catholics, pp. 278-279.

[71]Catholics, pp. 303-304. This fourth test is simply a variation on the second. Newman is not concerned with prejudices here as the context makes clear. The sentence immediately preceding is "Before he advances a step in his argument, he ought to prove his First Principle true". What Newman is objecting to here is the arbitrary imposition by a Protestant of his local first principles. This is bigotry but it is not prejudice.

[72]Curiously, McCarthy criticizes this test for failing to discriminate between true first principles and false first principles! (75) The problem with this is, of course, that the third test, as the context makes clear, is intended to distinguish first principles as a class from prejudices as a class. McCarthy wants the first and second tests to distinguish first principles from prejudices when they are designed to distinguish between true and false first principles: McCarthy wants the third test to distinguish between true and false first principles when it is intended to distinguish between first principles and prejudices.

[73]A glance at the list of first principles above will confirm this.

[74]If relative first principles are not prior to reason, it might be wondered why they are called first principles at all. The reason they are called first principles is that they function as such within a limited domain. Within the domain over which they range as first principles they are unquestionable.

[75]Grammar, p. 194. Except for some parenthetical remarks, McCarthy ignores the section on "Presumption" in the Grammar where Newman's most detailed account of first principles (outside Catholics) is to be found.

[76]Plantinga comes up with a strikingly similar list. What he calls the deliverances of reason include:
* the self-evident and its consequences
* basic perceptual truths (evident to the senses)
* certain memory processes
* certain propositions about other minds
* certain moral/ethical propositions. (93)

[77]McCarthy, pp. 81-82.

[78]McCarthy, pp. 130-151.

[79]In this section McCarthy comes close to seeing that the illative sense performs two distinct functions. One is extra-logical and concerned with first principles; the other is the architectonic faculty of inference. McCarthy thinks that the connection of the Noetic Faculty (or the illative sense in its extra-logical mode) with first principles denies their original character. But he is wrong in thinking this. It appears to be so only because he doesn't actually distinguish the intuitive and inferential functions of the illative sense. If first principles are arrived at inferentially then it is obvious that they are not original. But insofar as first principles are associated with the illative sense it is with the illative sense in its intuitive function rather than its inferential function. (This is true strictly only for absolute first principles; relative first principles may be derived inferentially.)

[80]McCarthy, p. 84.

[81]McCarthy, p. 87.

[82]McCarthy, p. 89, citing P.Flanagan, Newman, Faith, and the Believer, (London, 1946).

[83]McCarthy, p. 93.

314

[84]While it is true that Newman does not provide us with a set of necessary and sufficient conditions to enable us to distinguish true from false first principles, he does give us a set of pragmatic 'marks' which, while not conclusive, are nevertheless useful in helping us to decide on the truth of a given first principle.

[85]See the discussion of First Principles above.

[86]It will not do to rule out too quickly the notion that certain propositions may possess some characteristics which incline us to allow them to play a foundational role in our systems. Unless our linguistic systems are completely arbitrary it would seem plausible to suggest that the systems we possess are they way they are because certain propositions are inherently capable of playing a foundational role.

[87]This, of course, is very close to Collingwood's notion of an absolute presupposition but he gets no mention here. Strawson is mentioned. The citation is to "On Referring," Mind LIX (1950), 320-344.

[88]Here again, McCarthy is a little too quick. There are many places in the world where witchcraft is not yet defunct. The entire noetic structure of this linguistic system, complete with presuppositions and "unconditionally assertible proposotions" remains intact in some regions. See E.E. Evans-Pritchard, Witchcraft, Oracle, and Magic among the Azande, (Oxford, 1937).

[89]See "The Critics" in chapter three.

[90]See Toulmin's Human Understanding, 79-96.

[91]This seems to be a kind of double-aspect theory of certitude. Viewing a proposition in the cosy warmth of its presuppositional system, we regard it as certain; but seeing itg in the cold light of inter-systemic reality, we realize that we are really only entitled to have certitude in regard to it.

[92]Newman does not hold that our first principles are so luminous that they are present to our intellectual vision from birth. On the contrary, he claims, (with Collingwood) that it is only with great difficulty that we come to know our first principles. Once we entertain them, then we recognise them for what they are.

[93]D.H. Whittier, "Basic Assumption and Argument in Philosophy," The Monist, XLVIII, 1964.

[94]Whittier, pp. 489-490.

[95]Whittier, pp. 490-491.

[96]Cf. Plantinga's views on the relevance of arguments to basic beliefs.

[97]Whittier, p. 492.

[98]P.A.Schouls, "Communication, Argumentation, and Presupposition in Philosophy," Philosophy and Rhetoric, II, 1969.

[99]Schouls, p. 183.

[100]Schouls appeals to Whittier here in support of his claims.

[101]Schouls, p. 191.

[102]This seems a little too sweeping. Surely the presence of inconsistencies in one's noetic structure should lead one to modify it somewhat, not least by the modification or abandonment of one or more presuppositions.

[103]Schouls, p. 193, quoting from F.Waismann, "How I See Philosophy," in Contemporary British Philosophy, third series, ed. by H.D.Lewis (London,1956), pp. 482-486.

[104]J.King-Farlow, "On Making Sense in Philosophy (A Reply to Professor Peter Schouls)," Philosophy and Rhetoric, IV, 1971.

[105]There is an ambiguity in Schouls concerning 'understanding.' Understanding can mean either knowledge of the articulation of a system without necessarily being commited to it, or knowledge of the articulation of the system and, in addition, seeing why it is that the system as a whole is attractive, and thus, perhaps, accepting it. It is vital to distinguish these two senses of 'understanding.'

[106]G.Kodish, "Professor Schouls' Presuppositions," Philosophy and Rhetoric, IV, 1971, 48-54.

[107]It is difficult to see how someone can deny a basic presupposition if he doesn't even understand it! Here we have another reason to distinguish beteen understanding as a grasp of the inner workings of the system, and understanding as a grasp of the point of the system as a whole. If I understand that the basic presuppositions of a particular school are contradictories o f my own, then I understand those alien basic presuppositions. As a corollary, if two schools have totally distinct semantic notions, in what sense can they be concerned about the 'same thing'? In the case of radical semantic isolationism, it would be impossible to know that you were discussing the same thing.

[108]Achaval and Holmes, p. 88.

[109]Achaval and Holmes, p. 142; p. 146.

[110]Grammar, p. 321. See also, Catholics, p. 283; and Achaval and Holmes, p. 67.

[111]Grammar, p. 290.

[112]Grammar, p. 282.

[113]W.P.Ward, The Life of John Henry Cardinal Newman Based on his Private Journals and Correspondence, vol.2., (London, 1912), pp. 492-493.

[114]Gordon Huntington-Harper, Cardinal Newman and William Froude, F.R.S.: A Correspondence, (Baltimore, 1933.)

BIBLIOGRAPHY

Newman's Works

An Essay in Aid of a Grammar of Assent. Notre Dame:
University of Notre Dame Press, 1979.

The Idea of a University. New York: Image Books, 1959.

Lectures on the Present Position of Catholics in England. London: Longmans, Green, and Co., 1903.

The Philosophical Notebooks of John Henry Newman, eds.
A.J.Boekraad and H.Tristram. 2 vols. New York:
Humanities Press, 1970.

318

The Theological Papers of John Henry Newman on Faith
and Certainty, eds. H.M.Achaval and J.D.Holmes.
Oxford: Clarendon Press, 1976.

Fifteen Sermons Presented before the University of Oxford. London: Longmans, Green and Co., 1892.

Secondary Sources

Artz, J. "Newman and Intuition," Philosophy Today I
(1957), 10-16.

___. "Newman's Contribution to Theory of Knowledge,"
Philosophy Today, IV (1960), 12-25.

___. "Newman as Philosopher," International Philosoph-
ical Quarterly, XVI (1976), 266-287.

Bacchus, F. "Newman's Oxford University Sermons," The
Month, CXL (1922), 1-12.

_____. "How to Read the Grammar of Assent," The Month, CXLIII (1924), 106-115.

Bastable, J. D. "Cardinal Newman´s Philosophy of Belief," Irish Ecclestical Record LXXXIII (1953) 241-252; 346-351; 436-441.

_____. "The Germination of Belief within Probability according to Newman," Philosophical Studies (Irl.), XI (1961), 81-111.

_____. (ed.). Newman and Gladstone. Dublin: Veritas Publications, 1978.

_____. "Newman Publication," Philosophical Studies (Irl.), XXVI (1979), 204-209.

Blehl, V.F. John Henry Newman: A Bibliographical Catalogue of His Writings. Charlottesville (Virginia) 1978.

Boekraad, A.J. The Personal Conquest of Truth according to J.H. Newman. Louvain: Editions Nauwelaerts, 1955.

_____. "Newman's Argument to the Existence of God," Philosophical Studies (Irl.), VI (1956), 50-71.

_____. "Continental Newman Literature," Philosophical Studies (Irl.), VII (1957), 110-116.

_____. "The Personal Conquest of Truth," Louvain Studies,(1975), 136-148.

_____. "Grammar of Assent: Observations in the Margin," Newman Studien IX (1974) 206-218.

_____. "Newman Studies: Part I," Philosophical Studies, (Irl.), XX (1972), 185-202.

_____. "Newman Studies: Part II," Philosophical Studies, (Irl.), XXII (1974), 198-222.

_____., and Tristram, H. The Argument From Conscience to the Existence of God. Louvain: Editions Nauwelaerts, 1961.

Brickel, A.G. "Cardinal Newman's Theory of Knowledge," The American Catholic Quarterly Review, Bd. XLIII, (1918), 507-518; 645-653.

Browne, R.K. "Newman: Some Recent Books," The Month, CCXV (1963), 95-100.

Brunton, J.A. "The Indefectibility of Certitude," Downside Review, LXXXIII (1968), 250-265.

Burgum, E.B. "Cardinal Newman and the Complexity of Truth," Sewanee Review, XXXVIII (1930), 310-327.

Cameron, J.M. "The Logic of the Heart," The Listener, (1957), 51-52.

322

_____. The Night Battle. Baltimore: Helicon Press, 1962.

_____. "Newman and Locke: A Note on Some Themes in An Essay in Aid of a Grammar of Assent," Newman Studien IX (1974), 197-205.

_____. J.H. Newman. Vol. 72 of Writers and Their Works. London: 1956.

_____. "The Night Battle," The Listener, (1957), 15-16.

Carney, J.D. "Cogito Ergo Sum and Sum Res Cogitans." The Philosophical Review, LXXI (1962), 492-496.

Cavanagh, P.E. "The Doctrine of Assent of J.H. Newman," Unpublished Doctoral Dissertation. Philosophy Department, University of Notre Dame, 1964.

Collingwood, R.G. An Essay on Metaphysics. Oxford: Clarendon Press, 1940.

Collins, J. God in Modern Philosophy. Chicago: Henry
     Regnery Company, 1959.

_____. Philosophical Readings in Cardinal Newman.
     Chicago: Henry Regnery Company, 1961.

Coulson, J. "Belief and Imagination," Downside Review,
     XC (1972), 1-14.

Cronin, J.F. Cardinal Newman: His Theory of Knowledge.
     Washington: The Catholic University of America,
     1935.

D'Arcy, M.C. The Nature of Belief. Dublin: Clonmore and
     Reynolds Ltd., 1958.

_____. "The Genius of Newman: A Reply to E.Sillem,"
     Clergy Review, XLVIII (1963), 388-389.

Davis, H.F. "Newman on Faith and Personal Certitude,"
     Journal of Theological Studies, XII (1961),
     248-259.

Demos, R. "On Persuasion." The Journal of Philosophy, XXXIV (1932), 225-232.

Dessain, C.S. "Newman as a Philosopher," Tablet, CCVII (1956), 282.

_____. "Cardinal Newman on the Theory and Practice of Knowledge: The Purpose of the Grammar of Assent," Downside Review, LXXV (1957), 1-23.

_____. "Cardinal Newman's Papers," Dublin Review, CCXXXIV (1960), 291-296.

_____. "The Newman Archives in Birmingham," Newman Studien, III (1957), 269-273.

Evans, G.R. "Science and Mathematics in Newman's Thought," Downside Review, XCVI (1978), 247-260.

_____. "An Organon More Delicate, Versatile and Elastic: J.H. Newman and Whateley's Logic," Downside Review, XCVII (1979), 175-191.

Evans-Pritchard, E.E. Witchcraft, Oracle and Magic
among the Azande. Oxford: Clarendon Press,
1937.

Feigl, H. "De Principiis Non Disputandum Est." in Max
Black (ed.) Philosophical Analysis. Ithaca:
Cornell University Press, 1950.

Ferreira, M.J. Doubt and Religious Commitment: The Role
of the Will in Newman's Thought. Oxford: Clarendon Press, 1980.

Fey, W.R. Faith and Doubt: The Unfolding of Newman's
Thought on Certainty. Shepherdstown (West
Virginia): Patmos Press, 1976.

Ford, J.T. "Two Recent Studies on Newman," The Thomist,
XLI (1977), 424-440.

Frankfurt, H.G. "Descartes'Discussion of His Existence
in the Second Meditation." The Philosophical
Review, LXXV (1966), 329-356.

326

_____. Demons, Dreamers and Madmen. New York: Bobbs Merrill, 1970.

Froude, J.A. Short Studies on Great Subjects. New York: Charles Scribner and Co., 1871.

Griffin, J.R. Newman: A Bibliography of Secondary Studies. Front Royal, Va.: Christendom College Press, 1980.

Harper, G.H. Cardinal Newman and William Froude: A Correspondence. Baltimore: Johns Hopkins Press, 1933.

Hick, J. Faith and Knowledge. Ithica: Cornell University Press, 1957.

Hintikka, Jaakko. "Cogito Ergo Sum, Inference or Performance?" The Philosophical Review LXXI (1962), 3-32.

_____. "Cogito Ergo Sum as an Inference and a Performance." The Philosophical Review, LXXII (1963), 487-496.

Hogan, J.D. "Newman on Faith and Reason," Studies, XLII (1953), 132-150.

Holmes, J.D., and MacKinnon, D.M. (eds.). Newman's University Sermons. London: S.P.C.K., 1970.

Kaiser, F.J. The Concept of Conscience according to John Henry Newman. Washington: Catholic University of America Press, 1958.

Ker, I.T. "Newman on Truth," Irish Theological Quarterly, XLIV (1977), 67-78.

_____. "Recent Critics of Newman's A Grammar of Assent," Religious Studies, XIII (1977), 63-71.

King-Farlow, J. "On Making Sense in Philosophy (A Reply to Professor Peter Schouls)." Philosophy and Rhetoric, IV (1971), 42-54.

Klubertanz, G.P. "Where is the Evidence for Thomistic Metaphysics?" Revue Philosophique de Louvain, LVI (1958), 294-315.

Kodish, G. "Professor Schouls' Presuppositions." Philosophy and Rhetoric, IV (1971), 48-54.

Krausz, M. Critical Essays on the Philosophy of R.G. Collingwood. Oxford: Clarendon Press, 1972.

Lash, N. "The Notion of 'implicit' and 'explicit' reason in Newman's University Sermons: A Difficulty," Heythrop Journal, XI (1970), 48-54.

Lyons, J.W. Newman's Dialogues on Certitude. Rome: Catholic Book Agency, 1978.

McCarthy, G.D. "Religion and Certainty: John Henry Newman's Theory of First Principles." Unpublished Doctoral Dissertation. University of Pennsylvania, 1977.

Mavrodes, G. Belief in God. New York: Random House, 1970.

Mitchell, B. The Justification of Religious Belief. New York: Oxford University Press, 1981.

Naulty, R.A. "Newman's Dispute with Locke," Journal of the History of Philosophy, XI (1973), 453-457.

Newman, Jay. "Cardinal Newman's 'Factory-Girl Argument'," Proceedings of the American Catholic Philosophical Association, XLVI (1972), 71-77.

_____. "Cardinal Newman's Phenomenology of Religious Belief," Religious Studies, X (1974), 129-140.

_____. "Newman on the Strength of Beliefs," The Thomist, XLI (1977), 131-147.

_____. "Cardinal Newman on the Indefectibility of Certitude," Laval Theologique et Philosophique, XXXIV (1978), 15-20.

_____. "Newman on Love as the Safeguard of Faith," Scottish Journal of Theology, XXXII (1979) 139-152.

Pailin, D.A. The Way to Faith: An Evaluation of Newman's Grammar of Assent as a Response to the Search for Certainty in Faith. London: Epworth Press, 1969.

Petipas, H. "Newman's Personalism: A Precursor to Existentialism," American Benedictine Review, XVI (1965), 84-96.

Plantinga, A. "Reason and Belief in God." Unpublished Paper, University of Notre Dame, 1981.

Price, H.H. Belief. New York: Humanities Press, 1969.

Reardon, B.M.G. "Newman and the Psychology of Belief," Church Quarterly Review, CLVIII (1957), 315-332.

Robinson, J. "Newman's Use of Butler's Arguments." The
Downside Review, LXXVI (1958), 161-180.

Schiller, F.C.S. Problems of Belief. London: Hodder and
Stoughton, 1924.

Schouls, P.A. "Communication, Argumentation, and Presupposition in Philosophy." Philosophy and Rhetoric, II (1969), 183-199.

Sillem, E. "Cardinal Newman as a Philosopher: Notes on
Recent Work," Clergy Review, XLVIII (1963),
167-185.

_____. "Cardinal Newman's Grammar of Assent on Con-
science as a Way to God," Heythrop Journal, V
(1964), 377-401.

_____ (ed.). The Philosophical Notebook of John Henry
Newman. 2 Vols. New York: Humanities Press,
1969.

332

Steinberg, E. "Newman's Distinction between Inference and Assent." Unpublished Paper, Brooklyn College of City University of New York, 1983.

Toulmin, S. Human Understanding. Part I. Oxford: Clarendon Press, 1972.

Toohey, J.J. An Indexed Synopsis of the "Grammar of Assent". London: Longmans, Green and Co., 1906.

Verbeke, G. "Aristotelian Roots of Newman's Illative Sense," in J. D. Bastable (ed.), Newman and Gladstone, Dublin: Veritas Publications, 1978.

Ward, W.G. On Nature and Grace. London: Burns and Lambert, 1860.

Weinberg, J. "Cogito Ergo Sum: Some Reflections on Mr. Hintikka's Article." The Philosophical Review, LXXI (1962), 483-491.

Whittier, D.H. "Basic Assumption and Argument in Philosophy." The Monist, XLVIII (1964), 486-500.

Wicker, B. "Newman and Logic," Newman Studien, V (1963), 251-268.

Williams, M. Groundless Belief. New Haven, Connecticut: Yale University Press, 1977.

Zeno, O.M. "The Newman-Meynell Correspondence," Franciscan Studies, XII (1952), 310-348.

____. John Henry Newman: Our Way to Certitude. Leiden: E.J. Brill, 1957.

____. "An Introduction to Newman's Grammar of Assent," Irish Ecclesiastical Record CIII (1965), 389-406.